Praise for *When Your Parent Moves In*

"No stone unturned, this is the book to read before asking parents to move in. What's even more emotionally challenging than the process of sharing the same roof over your heads is the possibility that the living arrangement is not working, and you're now faced with the dreadful task of asking parents to move out. You'll never have to wonder if you did the right thing if you read this book now."

—Joy Loverde

Author of *The Complete Eldercare Planner: Where to Start, Which Questions to Ask, and How to Find Help* (Random House)

"I have been in the elder care arena for the past thirty-five years and I am always looking for good resource material. *When Your Parent Moves In* has an excellent ability to take you through the various steps needed when your parents or any other person you are finding yourself in the position of caring for need assistance, guidance, or direction. When it comes to making a move, this book is a clear guide. [It provides readers] with questions to ask and remains sensitive to maintaining the dignity and independence of the elderly who will be impacted by a move.

"This book explores the various issues regarding making the transition and understanding all the potentia̸   ̇ifications of a move, be it to a new home, living with oth̸   ̇embers, or moving into an institutional setting. The̸   ̇ in the back of the book are invaluable infor̸   ̇n and understanding."

—Marion S̸

Autho̸   ̇e Easier: Doctor
Marion̸.   ̇p You Care for an
Aging Lovea̸

President & Founder, Elder Health Resources of America, Inc.

www.DoctorMarion.com

Praise for *When Your Parent Moves In*

"Horgan and Block's book is timely and much needed for any family with aging parents. Clear, direct, and easy-to-understand language. This will be a must-read for my clients. . . ."

—Daniel O. Tully, Esq.

Former Assistant Attorney General,
State of Connecticut

"With my over twenty-five years of helping older persons and their families through Elder Law, I welcome *When Your Parent Moves In*. The authors use real-life studies and focused, practical questions to educate Baby Boom children. They help readers—especially "sandwich generation" members—analyze many relevant factors to determine if it is right for everyone involved to have a parent move in. They encourage respect throughout the process, but especially when the decision is for the parent not to move in.

This is an essential book for meaningful family discussions in these times when the economic downturn has reduced both available personal finances and government programs to fund long-term services. The authors show the value of working with experienced Elder Law attorneys, financial planners, and care managers who know local services, laws, and regulations."

—Timothy M. Vogel, Esq.

Senior Shareholder, Vogel & Dubois
Law Firm

Former Chair of the Elder Law Section of
the Maine State Bar Association

when your
parent
moves in

when your parent moves in

EVERY ADULT CHILD'S GUIDE TO LIVING WITH AN AGING PARENT

DAVID HORGAN

AND

SHIRA BLOCK, MA, PSYCHOLOGY AND COUNSELING

Avon, Massachusetts

Published by
Adams Media, a division of F+W Media, Inc.
57 Littlefield Street, Avon, MA 02322. U.S.A.
www.adamsmedia.com

ISBN 10: 1-60550-012-7
ISBN 13: 978-1-60550-012-6

Printed in the United States of America.

J I H G F E D C B A

Library of Congress Cataloging-in-Publication Data
is available from the publisher.

This publication is designed to provide accurate and authoritative
information with regard to the subject matter covered. It is sold with
the understanding that the publisher is not engaged in rendering legal,
accounting, or other professional advice. If legal advice or other expert
assistance is required, the services of a competent professional person
should be sought.
—From a *Declaration of Principles* jointly adopted by
a Committee of the American Bar Association
and a Committee of Publishers and Associations

Many of the designations used by manufacturers and sellers to distin-
guish their product are claimed as trademarks. Where those designations appear in this book and Adams Media was aware of a trademark
claim, the designations have been printed with initial capital letters.

To protect the privacy of those who have shared their stories, names
and sometimes genders have been changed.

This book is available at quantity discounts for bulk purchases.
For information, please call 1-800-289-0963.

In loving memory of Uncle Ed and Al.

—D.H.

In loving memory of
Sayes "Good-looking" Block
and Grandpa Carl.

—S.B.

contents

acknowledgments

This book would not have been possible without the willingness of many clients, subjects, and family members who candidly shared their stories so that others may learn, grow, and find peace in their own lives. Your openness and generosity is greatly appreciated. For those who have trusted us with stories that did not end up in the book, please know that your honesty and openness allowed us to add depth to our understanding of the complexity of this issue, and we are richer for it.

We would like to thank Andrea Norville at Adams Media for her guidance, good humor, and faith in the project, as well as Meredith O'Hayre for her insightful contributions and helpful suggestions. We would also like to thank Sheila Elmosleh for her precise copyediting, and Beth Gissinger and Jacquinn Williams for ensuring that we reach those who will benefit from reading this book. It is a great pleasure to be part of the Adams Media team.

From David Horgan:

I would like to thank my wife, Julie, and my sons, Andrew, Davis, and Cory. They are my life and my inspiration. I want to thank my mother-in-law and all my family for giving me the encouragement to explore new ventures.

I am fortunate to know the professionals at Senior Resource Center. They have helped me and my family and offered insight for *When Your Parent Moves In*. Anthony, David, and Kathy offered many hours of consultation and information from their years of helping adult children care for their parents.

I must also thank Shira Block for helping me turn an idea into an exceptional guide.

From Shira Block:

I would like to thank David Horgan for including me in this wonderful project and in his vision for this book.

I will be forever grateful to Ed Knappman, who responds to my effusiveness with, "Just doin' my job." You make the process—even when it's frustrating—fun. It is my great honor to work with you. Thank you for your faith in me and in this project.

I deeply thank Alan, my wonderful husband and soul mate, who has given me more love and support than I had ever hoped for, and who has allowed me to know what real love is. I would especially like to thank my beautiful, intelligent, and creative daughter, Aarin, who means everything to me. She has generously given up some of her mommy time so that I could write.

Ilana Katz, writer, musician, artist, friend, sounding board, and tireless supporter gets my special thanks for her constant friendship, encouragement, and endless input into this work.

You joined me every step of the way in the process and in my excitement. Your insight and knowledge of the industry is invaluable and you helped make the project that much more fun.

I consider the day I met the very talented Caitlin Moon a fortuitous one. Your ability to see the big picture and natural flow of communication and events has ensured that this book not only remains on track, but also tells a clear story in an authentic voice.

There are many people whose overall support and guidance help me believe in endless possibilities. David Claiborne, whose partnership and friendship has enriched my life on many levels; Brenda Edwards, whose love and counsel feels like a blessing; Deborah Mutschler, who expanded my ability to understand the intricacies of relationships and attach nuances to words, and taught me how to write; and Beth Rosenberg, whose wisdom and service to the underdog is a constant inspiration.

In addition, my mother, Barbara Block, who will end up on an ice floe in Alaska unless she shapes up (just kidding—Mom knows she will always have a home with me). Melissa Alves, David Block, Deborah Block—the funniest person I know—Piper Foreso, Ofelia Hodge, Julie Jacobs, Beth Ann Latsko, David McCormick, Di McCormick, Susan Sama, Jeff Schnepper, Nettie Scott, Dan Shanis—who made me feel like I could do anything—Doug Smullens, Joshua Smullens, and Rosa Ziv: Having all of you in my life makes it that much better.

And to all of you who are in the difficult position of caring for your family and parents. We are all in this together.

introduction

We are the Sandwich Generation. We are sitting between two generations needing care: our own children and our aging parents. Although it may feel, at times, that we are alone in this emotionally, financially, and logistically challenging situation, there are millions of us facing this responsibility.

We wrote this book because when we were faced with caring for our elderly parents in addition to our own families, we each fumbled through the process. While there are many books about caring for the elderly, not one addresses the problems that arise when deciding whether or not to blend several generations under one roof, let alone offers guidance on how to do so successfully.

The good news for you is that because of the difficulties we faced, we made it our mission to help you avoid making the same mistakes we did. We provide the necessary tools so that you can make the best decisions for your individual situation. By the time you finish this book, you will know how to decide if a loved one should move in, and how to make it work if you ultimately come to that decision.

When Your Parent Moves In will help you:

- Decide if having a loved one move in with you is the right decision
- Plan for the move
- Spell out rules and create healthy boundaries for your new living arrangement
- Expect the unexpected and learn how to roll with the changes
- Decipher your parent's financial position and best protect and manage his assets
- Create open dialogues
- Deal with difficult personalities
- Find balance (or something like it!)
- Preserve your core family unit

We wrote this book to shed light on the ups and down of what it means for you, your family, and your parent when you live together, and we hope *When Your Parent Moves In* will help you every step of the way.

Since you are reading this book, you are probably looking for help. Something is probably changing in the care needs of your parent and you are trying to manage this tumultuous time. For you, the time has come, and something needs to change. Maybe after taking The Moving-In Quiz in Chapter 2, you will decide to move your parent into your home. Maybe you will come to a different conclusion. Regardless of the change you ultimately make, the road to that decision should be paved with knowledge rather than a hasty or impulsive decision.

If you are considering moving your parent into your home, then the subsequent chapters in this book will give you a clear idea of how to decide if the move is right for you, and how to carry out your decision effectively. You will learn how to organize your parent's finances and plan the logistics of the move. You will read methods that other families have used to successfully integrate their parent into their new household. You will see how others have been able to preserve the peace within their family unit. And, you will learn how to prepare for the unexpected, which is inevitable when caring for the elderly.

If you have already moved your parent in, then this book will give you ideas for creating a stronger and more meaningful living arrangement. You will read lessons learned from families who have already gone through this kind of transition and made the move work for them. This book also includes many resources and organizations that specialize in assistance with eldercare issues. Although this book contains general eldercare tips, its focus is primarily on living with your parent.

When Your Parent Moves In is your guide to making the right decision about your parent's living situation and maneuvering through the ins and outs of this major life change so that the move can be a better, more fulfilling experience for you all.

David Horgan's Story

In 2004, my mother-in-law became too ill to live alone. We were emotionally unprepared for this because she had always been the matriarch of the family, the go-to person, and the core and pillar of the family structure. She was the hub around which all activities gravitated. Accepting that her health was failing was difficult for all of us. After a brief discussion, my wife and I came up with what we felt was the best solution: move Mom in with us. We made all the arrangements, completed the move, and before we knew it, Grandma was making pancakes for the kids in the morning before they left for school.

I am a practical guy. I make solid, level-headed, and educated decisions, especially when the outcome may affect my kids. My wife and I felt that moving Grandma in would benefit all of us. It was the right decision for our family, but our lack of foresight and planning (though I didn't realize how little prepared I was at the time) caused bumpy times that could have been avoided.

Years later, we are all settled into the new family structure and it is working. Looking back, though, I can see how we blindly stumbled into this monumental move. I remember saying to my wife that there should be some type of guide or manual to help families make this life-changing transition. There's so much to consider; there are so many things that you wouldn't think about that can have a profound effect on your life and your parent's.

Now, I have the knowledge, wisdom, input from the experts, and personal experience that I needed years ago to make this transition work. If you are considering having your dad or mom move in with you, I would urge you to read this book. It is comprehensive and necessary for an informed decision and a successful outcome.

When Your Parent Moves In is not my story, but a compilation of stories from dozens of families in which an elderly parent came to call his or her child's house home. For some people, moving in a parent may not be the best decision. For others, it can become a successful co-op of generations coexisting with respect and love.

Shira Block's Story

Six years ago I received a frantic call from my sister telling me our father had a stroke. I was shocked, because he had been fine the week before. Within minutes of seeing him in the hospital, it was clear that something was wrong. Despite my father's best efforts to appear normal, it was evident that his short-term memory was damaged. In addition, my father was now blind. That was his worst nightmare, and from that moment, none of our lives would ever be the same.

Because of medical complications, our father could no longer manage his life on his own. Therefore, my sister and I have spent the last six years handling our own lives while orchestrating and overseeing our father's very complicated life and finances. The insurance company viewed his short-term memory loss and blindness as an ongoing condition, rather than an acute illness, and would not cover full-time care. As if our devastation wasn't enough, we were now faced with financial hardships as we arranged for costly private home health care.

With limited resources, my sister and I began the very difficult conversation of how to effectively care for our father. We didn't want him to be alone, but he didn't need nursing care, just assistance, and was still quite independent. We thought assisted living would be perfect, but he vehemently disagreed. We discussed moving him in with one of us. However, he has a very strong personality and demands a level of attention that we could not meet with our children, husbands, careers, and independent lives. In addition, our father would never be happy in either of our homes. It wasn't an easy decision, but we decided that moving him in with either of us would have been a disaster. Because of the decision to keep him at home, we care take from a distance. It is complicated, a financial stretch, and at times feels inadequate, but it was the right decision for us.

At the same time that we were managing my father's care, my father-in-law's health was deteriorating. Ten years prior he battled throat cancer, and now the side effects of the chemotherapy and radiation were taking their toll.

My husband and I invited Carl to stay with us. Unfortunately, during our weeks of discussions and planning, Carl passed away. We were heartbroken, and still struggle with the sadness of knowing he died alone.

I don't believe there is a right or wrong answer or a good-child scenario and a bad-child scenario. We based our decision on our parents' and our family's needs.

When David Horgan came to me with his book idea, I thought it was a great one, especially in light of my personal experience combined with my sixteen years of professional experience as a life coach. My hundreds of clients have shared their stories with me over the years, many of whom ultimately offered their experiences for this book. Combining my professional and personal experience, I came to understand the details of what it takes to make the right decision whether to move a parent in, and if you do, how to give it the best chance of working. For Dave, moving his mother-in-law in was the right decision. For me, not moving my father in was the right decision. Despite some conflicting emotions that I still feel, I know it was the right decision for all of us.

The following chapters in this book take you through the decision-making process of families who, just like yours, are now struggling to make the right decision regarding their aging parents' care. You will get a glimpse into what you may experience if your parent moves in with you. There is no universal formula for success; there is, however, flexibility, adaptability, patience, and the desire to care for your parent as best you can—and those qualities go a long way. You can't fix everything, but you can learn to manage whatever comes your way.

chapter 1

when they can no longer care for themselves

IT USUALLY DOESN'T happen overnight. You don't wake up one day to discover that the person who held you when you were scared and crying, gave you snacks after school, and told you how special you were even when you felt the opposite is now unable to care for herself. It happens gradually. It's like the day you catch a glimpse of your teenager looking grown-up and wonder, "When did this happen? Wasn't it just last month that he was dragging a teddy bear across the floor, coming into our room at midnight asking, 'Can I sleep with you?'"

No matter how much we may want to fight the aging process, it will eventually creep up on all of us. Some of us will be fortunate enough to age with little impairment, while others will not be so lucky. If you are reading this book, your parent may be one of those faced with physical or mental deterioration and in need of your help. You are not alone. Seventy-six million baby boomers (that's approximately 30 percent of the population in the United States) are either in or are approaching retirement age. Most baby boomers still have elderly parents. According to the Penn State Research Institute, more than 40 percent of those boomer parents will need long-term care. According to *The Complete AARP Guide,* 80 percent of the care they receive will be done by family members. If you are anticipating taking on the responsibility of your parent's care, you are in good company.

Some positive news is that medical care has greatly improved over the decades, raising the life expectancy of Americans to seventy-seven years—the highest in history. The bad news is that the costs of eldercare are also at an all-time high, while insurance benefits and federal assistance are becoming more limited. It leaves us all asking the same question: How do we make it work?

Since you will likely end up caring for your parents, how do you do so without robbing them of their dignity? How do you take over the role of parenting your parents without ruining the relationship you spent a lifetime building? How do you help your parents, especially if your relationship has been tumultuous, without jeopardizing the peace and harmony of your own family?

Throughout this book, you will read families' stories as they share their experiences and how they coped and worked toward successfully blending several generations under one roof. The first story comes from Eric.

ONE FAMILY'S EXPERIENCE *Eric and Jon*

I hadn't visited my Dad, Jon, in a while, but we regularly spoke on the phone. When I finally made the trip to my childhood home, I was struck by the size of the house. My memories were of big doors, tables, sofas, rooms, and a bigger-than-life Dad. The actuality of the house and its contents (Dad included) were miniature by comparison.

Dad and I have always been close. He was a good man. Thirty years ago I may have bemoaned my strict upbringing; however, I am now proud to say my parenting is a close mirror to his. After Mom died eight years ago, Dad seemed to slow down, though he'd never admit it—he was too tough for that.

Now, I don't even recognize him as the man he used to be. His thin white hair, stooped posture, arthritic-bowed knees, and swollen, distorted knuckles belie the robust man I knew. Rheumatoid arthritis has taken its toll. Even his nails have changed—gone are the oil-stained fingernails that mom complained about at mealtime. He loved car mechanics, but hasn't touched a car in years.

Watching him slowly crumble was devastating. I hate the fact that when we walk he holds my arm, because my Dad doesn't, or shouldn't, need anyone to lean on. In addition to his physical deterioration, we got the news that he had bone cancer. That, coupled with his severe arthritis, made it close to impossible for him to live on his own. I could barely deal with the news. I had once admired his strength; now he was frail and weak and needed me to care for him. I felt frightened and unprepared, and I just wanted my old dad back.

Jon's deterioration and inability to care for himself was a shock to his son, Eric. Eric loved his father and had a difficult time letting go of the strong, take-charge man who raised him. Eric was faced with a role reversal; he must now parent his parent. He worried that he didn't know how to care for his father, that he would somehow harm or disappoint him, that his father would become angry when he broached the subject of the move, and that the move would disrupt Eric's own life.

In addition, Eric's father was emotionally frail, from his own multitude of ailments and the recent loss of his wife.

Eric felt paralyzed by his father's show of emotion because he had absolutely no idea how to deal with it. He had never seen his father vulnerable.

Taking on the role of caretaker is difficult under any circumstances. This is especially true when caring for your parent because of the long history; some of your history is good and maybe some of it more challenging. Even an eldercare expert may have a difficult time caring for his own parent. Wading through your own emotions, your parent's needs, and eldercare options is daunting. Regardless, you can make an informed decision. Gather information; make a plan; set some rules; get help. And, most importantly: Find the proper balance between your parent's needs and your own. After all, your own needs include the needs of your entire family as well as your career.

The good news is that there is help available, maybe even more than you are aware of. When approaching the difficult process of caring for your parent, remember that mental preparation is key. Start off on the right foot and keep the following in mind.

Accept Your New Role as Caretaker

Once you make the decision to have your parent move into your home, you must accept and embrace it. Imagine a six-year-old going to the doctor for a vaccine. One way or another, the child is getting a shot. She can get it the hard way—by kicking and screaming—or the easy way—by accepting it. The outcome remains the same, but attitude determines how painful the event is for everyone involved. Keep a good attitude, accept your decision, and do the best you can.

Accept the Inconsistency of Your Parent's Condition

Don't use the inconsistency of your parent's condition as an out or postponement for taking over the role of caretaker: "My mom doesn't need supervision; she only forgets to take her medication once in a while." That once in a while is what you need to watch out for. Forgetting to take her insulin or taking too much blood-thinner medication could have disastrous effects.

Or maybe you say to yourself, "Dad is just fine; he is just a little tired every now and then. Aren't we all?" The key is to be mindful of how consistently and effectively your parent can perform basic self-care tasks. (See Chapter 5, Managing and Protecting Your Parent's Assets, for more details.) Throughout life, people grow, mature, and age unevenly. Maybe your parent is still mentally sharp, but is experiencing physical deterioration. Examine the areas in which your parent needs assistance and determine the best way to help. Don't be lulled into a false sense of security if the need only presents itself occasionally. Once your parent can no longer consistently take care of himself, you will most likely have to step in and lend a hand. The hard decision will be whether or not your parent is capable of living on his own. That is something to address with careful consideration.

Broach the Subject

The quiz in Chapter 2 will help you determine if having your parent move in with you is the best course of action for your family. However, even before you make your final decision, it makes sense to begin thinking about how you would broach the subject with your parent.

You may have a clear idea of how you would like to care for your parent and step immediately into action. That's fine when you are coaching a basketball game, but not when you are initiating one of the most difficult conversations you will have with your parent. In essence, you are implying that she can no longer care for herself and that you are thinking of taking away her authority, responsibility, and decision making.

Imagine if someone said to you, "I don't think you are able to drive anymore. I'll pick you up on Saturdays and take you where you need to go." or, "I'm taking over your finances—you aren't handling them well." You would not like it. In fact, you'd probably hate it, and maybe even resent it. You would probably reject the "help." Your parent is no different. However, there are ways of delivering this unwelcome but necessary message while opening a dialog that will be helpful to everyone. The following sections outline seven ways to improve your chances of having your parent truly hear your message of love, concern, and desire to help.

Act Before an Emergency

If possible, you should try to initiate a conversation before an emergency, not in reaction to one. This will allow you to have a more calm conversation. You wouldn't want to tell your mother she can no longer drive in response to a car accident. This can feel like a punishment, and it will put your mother in a position to deflect any perceived blame.

It is more helpful to have the conversation when an immediate outcome or decision isn't crucial or when you have time to come up with solutions. But what happens if you are too late and already have to react to a crisis? Read through the following sections and keep in mind your parent is probably shaken up by what has occurred, so be doubly sensitive.

Give It Time to Sink In

Give your parent time to mull over what you have discussed. For instance, you can start with, "Mom, I have been concerned that your peripheral vision isn't that great anymore. Maybe you should start to think about alternatives to driving. I found out that there is a local shuttle service that can take you anywhere you want. I would be happy to pick you up on weekends and we can go grocery shopping together. We'll find a solution—you won't be stranded. I know that this is a new idea for you, and it might take you a little time to get your mind around it. Think about it, and we'll talk again in a few days."

After you have given your parent several days to consider your suggestion, you can casually approach the topic again with, "Do you remember our discussion about the shuttle service? I've been thinking about it and I'd love to try it out. Why don't we take it this weekend and go shopping together?" Offering to go with her may alleviate any anxiety she feels around trying something new. If she isn't open to the idea, you can discuss the possibility of incorporating her errands into your schedule, such as creating a routine of picking her up on Saturdays to take her grocery shopping. You can make the trip a pleasant experience for her, not a punishment.

Whether or not she proclaims, "Yes! I am ready to give up my car!" you can still help her get used to the idea while making a smooth transition. Your presence will show her she is not alone.

Make the Conversation a Two-Way Street

Be sure to include your parent in the conversation. Don't dictate—this is supposed to be a dialogue.

Take a moment to think about how your parent must feel; fast-forward thirty years and imagine your son or daughter telling you what's best for you and what you should do. How would you feel? Your parent has been making her own decisions for decades. Regardless of her current level of clarity or capacity, she will not only want to be part of the discussion and decision-making process, but she also deserves to be part of it. After all, it is her life you are talking about. This isn't a conversation that your parent can easily have. When broaching the subject, remember how difficult this topic can be.

Listen and respond to every concern your parent brings up, no matter how farfetched it may seem to you. If your mother claims moving her cats into your house will be too upsetting for them, consider that the cats may just be a focal point for her anxiety. Remember, your parent is faced with a major and irreversible life change; she will understandably be anxious. Work together whenever possible to brainstorm solutions. Your parent will feel more comfortable if she is part of the decision, rather than feeling steamrolled.

Also, ask your parent to help you come up with solutions rather than delivering the outcome. Ask, "You seem to be lonely and having a difficult time around the house. I can't help but worry that it is too much for you. What do you think would be the best solution?" Listen to your parent and hear what she is telling you.

Redirect the Conversation

The book *Caring for Your Parents: The Complete AARP Guide* suggests you bring up the conversation by directing the conversation toward yourself first. For example, if you are concerned about your mother's eyesight, don't say, "Mom, you are blind as a bat and should give up your driver's license." Try, "I have been noticing that I have been having a difficult time reading street signs at night. How about you? I'm getting my eyes checked in a couple weeks. We could go together." Or, "Jill and I have been thinking about making out a will. I don't like to think about those things, but it seems like a good idea. Mom, do you have one?" Look for a way to align yourself with your parent.

Be Clear about Why You're Concerned

Remind your parent of your motivation for having the conversation. You can never be too reassuring. Remind your parent that you love her and only want what's best. "Mom, we are having this conversation because you have fallen twice in the last two weeks. We love you and want you to be safe." Make sure you have a sensible reason for moving your parent in. "You are getting older and you shouldn't be alone" may work for some, but not for someone else who has a full social life.

Be Persistent

Be willing to have the same conversation several times. Regardless of age, it is difficult to retain information that goes against what you believe or want to hear. We tend to shut down or dismiss news that could disrupt our lives or require radical change—our minds try to make it go away. Not only is your parent naturally tuning out new and threatening ideas, but she may also struggle with a waning memory that may necessitate repeating the conversation at a later date. Be patient; give your parent a chance to absorb the discussion then try again. After a few times, your parent will realize that the conversation will not disappear and will begin to retain it. This is another reason why it is a good idea to have the conversation before an emergency strikes.

Make Your Parent's Home Safe in the Meantime

Ensure the safety of your parent's home until you both agree on the next steps. Here are a few stop-gaps to consider while you and your parents come to a decision:

- Would your parent benefit from handrails and nonslip mats in the bathroom?
- Should you tack down loose carpet edges?
- Should you remove any throw rugs?
- Can you move your parent's bedroom to the first floor?
- Would extra lighting in hallways make it easier for your parent to get around?
- Is clutter making your parent's house difficult to navigate? With your parent's help, can you remove or reorganize any items that he might trip on?

Think about the specific ways your parent's home may be unsafe and brainstorm ways to make it safer until you determine the correct course of action for care.

Decide on Timing of the Move

Your job as caretaker requires you take a look at your parent's situation and make the best decision for him. Don't make a move that will disrupt and affect your parent's life until it is necessary.

Experts believe that it is in the best interest of most senior citizens to stay in their own home for as long as safely possible. Just because your mother passes away doesn't necessarily mean the solution to your father's sadness or loneliness is to remove him from his home. A rushed decision may just compound the feeling of loss and helplessness; people feel a great deal of comfort from being in familiar surroundings. Your parent has routine interactions with the mailman, neighbors, or store clerks. He knows where to go and what to expect. People grow attached to possessions and pets, and disrupting that can have a psychologically detrimental effect which can impact health. Talk to a therapist or your parent's physician to determine when the timing is right.

Consider these alternatives to a quick decision to move:

- Hire a visiting nurse or aide if your parent needs some help with self-care.
- Enlist the help of friends and family to stop by on a regular basis to emotionally help your parent through a tough spot. Just make sure the visits are consistent.
- Hire a housekeeper or take on the task yourself if your parent has trouble keeping his house clean.
- Look into Meals on Wheels (*www.mowaa.org*) if your parent can no longer cook and you are concerned about nutrition.
- Have volunteers from local groups come and visit.
- Look into shuttle services for the elderly to help with transportation. Remember, your parent's autonomy is crucial to his dignity and psychological well-being. Your parent's emotional well-being can directly affect his health.

- Have your parent spend weekends with you.
- Enroll your parent at a local senior center. They are generally free and have many social and cultural activities.
- Use Life Alert necklaces (*www.LifeAlert.com*) if you fear your parent may fall.

Be Prepared for the Fallout

The moment you broach the subject of living arrangements or additional care with your parent is the moment that role reversal begins to take place. Don't be surprised if both you and your parent have a difficult time adjusting. That is exactly what happened with Lisa and her mother, Marion.

ONE FAMILY'S EXPERIENCE *Lisa and Marion*

Lisa's life seemed to grow a little more hectic since she took a more active role in caring for her mother, Marion. Mornings at Lisa's were a hectic blend of feeding the kids, packing lunches, and making sure homework was in its appropriate backpack. After her kids were off to school, Lisa would then stop by her mother's on the way to work, to check in on her. Marion was a little less mobile these days due to her fractured pelvis from a fall several months earlier. Lisa would remind her mom to use her cane and to be extra careful on the stairs. Lisa and her husband, Robert, had been discussing moving Marion in with them, but were not ready to broach the subject.

One morning Lisa arrived at her mother's to find her walking around without her cane. Marion was under strict orders to use the cane to prevent another fall. Lisa retrieved the cane from her mom's room and reminded her to use it. Marion was not happy as Lisa gave her strict instructions. Marion didn't want to admit that she was having difficulty balancing. She often referred to the cane as "that damn thing" and made comments like, "I'm fine, I don't need it all the time."

Little by little, the dynamics between Marion and Lisa became more challenging and uncomfortable. Marion was supposed to attend three weeks of physical therapy. She went twice and stopped. She gave numerous excuses and didn't think she needed more PT. Lisa found herself in an ongoing dialogue that Marion equated to lecturing and scolding. She was now in charge, and Marion was the rebellious child.

As time went on, the relationship between Lisa and Marion grew more tense. Lisa became adamant in trying to "guide" Marion into making the right decisions. She began treating her like a bad child. Marion resented the situation and began to withdraw. She wouldn't answer the phone when Lisa called, and tried to convince her to stop coming by in the morning. Lisa and Marion both felt lost and depressed by their deteriorating relationship.

There is an old saying: One mother can care for seven children, yet seven children can't care for one mother. It may be an old saying, but it still rings true. The truth is a mother has a clear and expected role. The mother raised the children from birth and has always been the caretaker. The children, on the other hand, have a different role—to learn and grow and be taken care of by the mother. Anything short of that can bring about resistance on both sides, especially for the parent who has lost her status as head of the household.

Imagine if you were a manager of a department at work for a long time, but suddenly your subordinate of twenty-five years is now telling you what to do. It would probably make you want to quit. In the previous example, Marion's way of quitting was to avoid her daughter.

Although you may feel you know what is best for your mother, remember the sensitivity of the situation and whenever possible give her room to make decisions for herself. Your job is to keep her safe; however, in many cases, the final decision is up to her.

Treating mom like a bad child—even if she is acting like one—will only bring about difficulties and alienation on both sides. Whenever possible, leave your parent with as much control over her life as you safely can. It will make life easier for all of you.

Lessons Learned

When your parent can no longer care for himself, your life will invariably change. Whether you take on the role of full-time, live-in caretaker or part-time caretaker you can expect not only a slew of tasks, but also intense emotions. Moving your parent into your home has far-reaching consequences, which will be laid out in the subsequent chapters. Remember:

- ❏ Make an informed decision, and prepare as best you can. Families that made the move work are the ones that made the decision for the right reason (see Chapter 2 for more details).
- ❏ Make a plan up front (see Chapters 3, 4, 5, and 6).
- ❏ Have calm conversations and try to come up with decisions together.

❑ Remember to be patient with your parent. He is facing a big life transition.

❑ Treat your parent with empathy (see Chapter 9 for more details), and forgive. Forgive what? Mistakes. Whose? Everyone's. To err is human, and humans err a lot.

chapter 2
the moving-in quiz

WOULDN'T IT BE GREAT if there was a quick and easy way to decide if your parent should move in with you? Unfortunately, there's not; the crystal ball won't work here. The good news is that even though there is no 100% accurate forecast, there are clear signs, good and bad, that can help steer you to the best answer. However, ignoring these signs can send you stumbling in the wrong direction while making one of the biggest decisions of your life.

Are you contemplating moving your mother-in-law into your home to make your spouse happy? Do you consider it a good investment to move your father in because he will help pay for an addition on your house? How about inviting old Aunt Millie to move in because you want a live-in babysitter? Maybe you feel pressured by your siblings because you are the one with the big house? Have you thought, "I'll move Grandpa in for a year or so, and if it doesn't work, I'll move him out"? These motivations are just a few indications that you may be heading toward a decision that could leave you and your family unprepared for the long-term reality of what it means to have an elderly relative move in. Making a good decision requires an honest look at your relationship with your parent, your motivation for considering the move, and the ultimate impact it may have on everyone involved.

The Moving-In Quiz illuminates blind spots in your decision making as well as potential reasoning flaws and traps. However, don't respond to the statements in The Moving-In Quiz the way you think you should; answer honestly. If you really don't want your mother-in-law to move in with you, be prepared to say so and discuss why. It is a waste of energy to try to hide your feelings; they will eventually surface. Bringing up potential obstacles before they become real-life problems gives you a chance to find solutions or compromises before there's a disaster, not after.

After taking The Moving-In Quiz, you may conclude that moving your parent in with you isn't the right decision after all. That doesn't make you a bad person, and it doesn't mean you don't love your parent. It just means that you will find a different decision that works for everyone. If the move isn't right for you and your family, then it ultimately won't work for your parent either, even if she doesn't immediately see it that way. Moving your parent in with you has the best chance of succeeding when the move works equally well for everyone involved.

The Moving-In Quiz

The Moving-In Quiz is the compilation of dozens of families' experiences moving an elderly parent in with them. Their overall successes and challenges were compared to their attitudes, underlying motivations, health of the parent, and strength of their core family relationship. Even though each family is unique and has their own set of issues and concerns, there are common themes for families who successfully integrated their parent into their home and for those who didn't. The quiz was born from comparing and categorizing these commonalities.

The goal of The Moving-In Quiz is to help you identify your underlying motivations for contemplating moving your parent into your home. Are your motives similar to those who had success stories? Or are they similar to those who consider the new living arrangement a constant struggle? You'll find out. Remember, the quiz will not give you the final answer, though it can make it easier for you to decide. When it comes right down to it, you and your family must make the decision and then live with the consequences, both good and bad.

Take The Moving-In Quiz when you have time to focus, rather than rushing through while you are making dinner or watching TV. Many have found taking the quiz and reading the analysis sections with a spouse to be very helpful. Read each section, stop, put the book down, discuss it, and come back tomorrow and review the next section.

How It Works

The Moving-In Quiz is divided into seven sections with five statements per section. Select a number from 1–5 for each statement that best reflects your feelings. One indicates "Never" and five indicates "Always." Once you have completed the quiz, add up your numbers for each section then divide by 5. That is your average for the section. After you have completed each section, read the analysis.

SECTION I: IDEALISM VERSUS REALISM

How often do the following apply?

1 Never **2** Almost Never **3** Sometimes **4** Almost Always **5** Always

___ As sad as it is, the move may be short term because of Dad's health.

___ This could be a big change for us, but at least we'll have a live-in babysitter.

___ We take family vacations together every year and we all get along great. Moving Mom in shouldn't be much different.

___ If I can handle my boss, husband, the house, two kids, and a dog, I can certainly handle Dad moving in.

___ We have a big house with plenty of space. Mom will have her own room, bathroom, and kitchenette. We won't even know she is there half the time.

Total: ___ / 5 = ___

SECTION II: GUILT

How often do the following apply?

1 Never **2** Almost Never **3** Sometimes **4** Almost Always **5** Always

___ Why am I the only one who steps up to the plate? If I don't take care of Mom, no one will.

___ Dad refuses to go into an assisted-living facility or even let us send a home health aide to see him. What choice do I have?

___ My spouse doesn't say it, but I know he/she expects me to take care of his/her mother. I don't want to upset anyone, so I'll just go along and try to make the best of it.

___ I can't abandon my parent. I couldn't live with myself if I did.

___ I know my mother thinks I don't care about her. That's not true, but she is always trying to make me feel bad.

Total: ___ / 5 = ___

SECTION III: FINANCIAL MOTIVATION

How often do the following apply?
1 Never **2** Almost Never **3** Sometimes **4** Almost Always **5** Always

___ Moving Dad in will be good for our family because he will help with our bills, and maybe even contribute to the addition we want to put on our house.

___ I don't trust my brother with Mom's money. If she lives here, we can at least oversee her finances and help her out.

___ We can't afford an assisted-living facility or home health care.

___ I don't want Dad to use up all his money for a nurse or home health care.

___ Assisted-living facilities are a waste of money; they charge thousands—and for what?

Total: ___ / 5 = ___

SECTION IV: SHAKY CORE-FAMILY FOUNDATION

How often do the following apply?
1 Never **2** Almost Never **3** Sometimes **4** Almost Always **5** Always

___ If I take care of my mother-in-law, maybe my spouse will appreciate me.

___ My spouse made all the decisions and I am just going along with it. I won't rock the boat. Besides, this is what he/she wants. I'm just keeping my mouth shut.

___ It just seems as if it is happening around me.

___ My marriage is so shaky; I could use the support and company.

___ I can't talk to my spouse about how I feel about the move. He/she just gets angry and it causes too many problems.

Total: ___ / 5 = ___

SECTION V: IMPATIENCE

How often do the following apply?
1 Never **2** Almost Never **3** Sometimes **4** Almost Always **5** Always

___ We have to make the decision *right now*. What's there to talk about? Let's move Mom in and work out the details later. I can always call her doctor if there is a problem.

___ After Dad moves in, if it doesn't work out, one of my siblings can take a turn.

___ I've already scheduled the movers and arranged for storage. I don't want to disrupt the schedule.

___ If we don't do this now, we'll have to pay for a nurse to come in and look in on Mom.

___ I want to handle all this before we go away on vacation (or start a new job, have a baby, and so on).

Total: ___ / 5 = ___

SECTION VI: ADULT-CHILD STANCE

How often do the following apply?
1 Never **2** Almost Never **3** Sometimes **4** Almost Always **5** Always

___ This is my home and family with my rules; he'll be a guest here. I hope he will be able to respect that.

___ I'll show through example how parenting should be done. He'll have to respect me when he sees me raising my own kids.

___ Considering what a bad mother she was, she should be grateful that I am willing to take care of her. If not, we'll just have to move her out.

___ This will give me and Dad a chance to repair our relationship. Besides I'm sure he'll mellow with age.

___ Dad expects me to take care of him. What else can I do? I don't have much choice.

Total: ___ / 5 = ___

QUIZ RESULTS FOR SECTION I

Section I, Idealism Versus Realism, identifies how realistic you are in regard to the potential impact moving an aging parent in with you will have. If you scored an average of three or higher, you may be glossing over what the move will mean for you and your family. An average of two or less may indicate that you have a good balance of realism and idealism, which could ultimately help you through the unexpected and difficult aspects of bringing your parent into your family structure.

STATEMENT 1

As sad as it is, the move may be short term because of Dad's health.

Regardless of a parent's degree of health or illness, do not plan a move under the premise that it will be short term. You can't predict a person's lifespan. Most people know someone who received a grim prognosis but then shocked all of the doctors with a miracle of many more years. When considering a move, think long term. You need to be realistic about Mom or Dad's health, but you don't want to be waiting for the end rather than enjoying your time together. Maybe the end will come soon, maybe it won't; there is no way of knowing, and it will not serve you well to make a decision based on unpredictable timing.

If you decide to move your parent in fueled by the expectation that the living arrangement would last only a few months, you may end up feeling frustrated and then guilty over your frustration when the arrangement lasts for years.

STATEMENT 2

This could be a big change for us, but at least we'll have a live-in babysitter.

In most cases, an elderly parent moves in because she is less-than-capable of self-care. Although your parent can participate in family activities, and may even watch your children from time to time, childcare should not be a major part of the decision-making process. Wishing, even a little, for added help around the house may be disappointing as your parent continues to age and becomes less able. Your parent is moving in so you can take care of her, as well as to be part of the family, not to care for your children, regardless of their own hopes or expectations to the contrary.

Additionally, take into consideration the time it will take for you to care for your parent. You won't feel so helped when you're dealing with doctor appointments, needs of the parent, loss of spousal alone time, and change in routines and family dynamics.

STATEMENT 3

We take family vacations together every year and we all get along great. Moving Mom in shouldn't be much different.

If you make a long-term decision based on short-term visits and vacations, you are making a decision based on faulty information. During short visits and vacations, most people are on company behavior. They can keep personality quirks and annoying habits at bay and they show tolerance and patience for the difficult traits of others. It is easy to get along when you are not burdened with daily chores and work. On vacation, you may have maid service, restaurants instead of cooking, stress-free days, and usually a separate space at the end of the day. The overall harmony you experience on vacations can't be easily recreated in day-to-day routines, stresses, and wear and tear of everyday life. What is tolerable for a week or two in a beautiful, relaxed vacation setting can be a nightmare under the pressures of everyday life.

You may be shocked to see how different it actually is once your parent is living with you. With a parent, you add emotional baggage as well as the possibility of another adult (consciously or unconsciously) vying for control of the house. Now add illness, dependency, and increasing care needs and it can be even more difficult. There is no real way to judge a long-term living situation by looking at short-term visits. If you want a real feel for what the living arrangement may be like, invite your parent to stay with you for a trial period of several months. You will have a chance to test the waters without the pressure of a permanent decision.

STATEMENT 4

> If I can handle my boss, husband, the house, two kids, and a dog, I can certainly handle Dad moving in.

The old adage, if you want something done, give it to a busy person is usually true. However, this is not the case when the busy person is already over her head with responsibilities. Just because you manage to juggle work, marriage, kids, household responsibilities, and extended family obligations, doesn't automatically mean you have the time or emotional capacity to squeeze in the daunting task of caring for an aging parent. Is your family on the brink of being overburdened? Will this send you over the edge? This is not about your parent requiring too much care; even the most supremely organized and competent person can eventually reach her limit. Be honest and assess your situation.

Many already-overwhelmed families who made the decision to move in a parent were not upset about the parent moving in, but were surprised or frustrated by what he brought into their lives. For example: "I love Dad and having him here, but what I can't take is the dog, the old furniture in my house, his stuff in my bathroom, all the medicine in my cabinets, and his friend Ed who comes over every Saturday night to play cards and expects me to wait on him hand and foot." When you bring your father into your house, he does not come alone. He brings along all of his stuff—the physical and the emotional—his friends, and his pets, and it is all added responsibility that you and your family will have to manage.

STATEMENT 5

> We have a big house with plenty of space. Mom will have her own room, bathroom, and kitchenette. We won't even know she is there half the time.

This may make sense in theory, but in actuality it has very little truth for most families. Imagine Grandma spent most of the day alone in her room or in the house. At around 6:00 P.M., your family starts trickling in. Of course she wants to be with everyone to catch up on the events of the day. Of course she wants to sit down for dinner with the family—she doesn't really want to eat alone. After a good meal together, the family retires to the living room to talk, watch TV, and just hang out. Of course she wants to be part of the group; this is why she moved in—to be part of the family. Although Grandma will have her own space, she does not want to feel banished to it.

In addition, when she left her own house or apartment and moved in with you, she became a permanent member of the household and will always be around. You are in for a surprise if you move your parent in thinking she would stay in her room or in the newly built addition.

If you consider your parent a guest, you are likely to feel a constant sense of invasion—as though you have a guest who won't leave. It is your home, and the rules are ultimately yours to make. However, if you need or want family alone time, you will have to ask for it. Your parent is not a mind reader, and when you require private time you will have to communicate that clearly and kindly. When Mom moves in you may have to reorganize the family routine to protect the down time that just happened naturally before the move.

QUIZ RESULTS FOR SECTION II

Section II identifies if you are making a decision out of guilt. Guilt is a tricky emotion and, at times, guilt can be so overwhelming it skews your ability to make a good decision. Guilt also creates a feeling of urgency, tempting you to rush into action just to alleviate the emotional pain and stress associated with it. In addition to blinding you into thinking you have little choice in how you care for your parent, guilt can also make you feel like a bad person for having your own needs. You can't easily will guilt away; however, you can weaken its hold by talking about how you feel, getting support, and learning when your decisions are motivated by unhealthy emotions. A guilt-driven decision rarely brings a good result.

If you scored an average of three or higher, you may be walking into a minefield of guilt leading to resentment, frustration, and the potential breakdown of your own well-being.

Feelings of guilt often develop into anger, causing emotional blowups, tension, and serious arguments once your parent moves in. An average of two or less may indicate that you have balanced what you want with healthy feelings of responsibility toward your family.

STATEMENT 1

Why am I the only one who steps up to the plate? If I don't take care of Mom, no one will.

Sadly, when a parent becomes ill or dependent, many family members become suspiciously unavailable. One person, often an adult child or a close relative, seems to take on the huge responsibility of primary care. Trying to force siblings or relatives who can't or won't help will get you nowhere. Guilt can make you think that you are the only one who can care for your parent, that you have no choice but to move your parent in. Don't let guilt determine your decisions. Social workers, therapists, counselors, and others who have experience in working with families caring for elderly parents can be a great help. Look through the many resources in this book as well as online. Make some calls. Get support to help alleviate guilt you may be feeling. You will not only improve your overall well-being, you will also psychologically free yourself to make a more balanced, educated decision.

If you do feel that you have no choice but to move your parent in yet can accept the situation rather than feeling pressured by it, you will have an easier time with the move. There is a difference between family obligation and guilt. Obligation can steer you toward caring for you parent. However, guilt keeps you from doing so lovingly. Relax and welcome your parent with heartfelt sentiments and you will make it easier for your parent and your family. The final living arrangements will be the same; however, the road to a new working family unit will be dramatically different.

STATEMENT 2

Dad refuses to go into an assisted-living facility or even let us send a home health aide to see him. What choice do I have?

How would you feel if you were told that you were half the person you used to be? How would you feel if you were told you can never drive again? How would you feel if you were told you must get rid of your dish collection, most of your furniture, your dog, and move out of the house you love? How would you feel if you were told that not only do you have to move, but that someone else was going to pick where you live? How would you feel if someone you trust tells you something about yourself that you don't believe—that you are not capable of living on your own anymore? How about if someone told you that you will have a stranger in your house taking care of you? Most likely, you would be outraged. So is your parent.

Before you write off other options for care, find out (if you can) why your father doesn't want to move into an assisted-living facility or why he becomes angry at the suggestion of a home health care worker. You might be surprised that your parent's fears, attitude, and concerns are exactly what yours would be under the same circumstances. Maybe the immediate no was because he was in shock over the conversation. Maybe he associates assisted-living facilities with a nursing home—a place where, in the past, people typically went to die. Maybe he has no idea that an assisted-living facility can entail independent living with available services, not a crowded living situation where he will have a roommate. Maybe he just can't accept that he isn't as he used to be, and just wants to be left alone.

Before you write off your parent's fears and apprehensions as irrational, talk to him and find out why he is uncomfortable. You may be surprised to find his position is more reasonable than you thought. Also consider visiting a facility you have in mind. Maybe seeing a place for himself will alleviate fears and hesitation. Many assisted-living facilities are beautiful, warm, and welcoming.

If you make the decision to move in a parent from the standpoint of "What else am I supposed to do? Dad won't move," you may feel angry and have a difficult time lovingly integrating him into the family. You may feel put upon and pressured into action.

If you take the time to find out the reason behind your parent's refusal or hesitancy, you may have an easier time showing compassion for him, which will make it easier to transition him into your home.

STATEMENT 3

My spouse doesn't say it, but I know he/she expects me to take care of his/her mother. I don't want to upset anyone, so I'll just go along and try to make the best of it.

It is almost impossible to permanently hide your feelings. If you invite your parent to move in with you when it is not something you want to do, you are setting yourself and your family up for a difficult time—eventually your feelings will come out. Many of the spouses interviewed who went along with the decision but were not truly behind it ended up depressed or angry with the housemate parent, the family, or the other spouse. This was especially true if the majority of care taking also fell on his shoulders.

However, those who actively agreed to move in an elderly parent and learned to accept the new living arrangement were able to move past feeling upset about the decision. Do not think that you are avoiding conflict by not rocking the boat. On the contrary, you are setting yourself and your family up for a lot of hurt feelings and frustrations down the road. Talk with your spouse now, even if it's difficult, and save yourself the heartache later.

STATEMENT 4

> I can't abandon my parent. I couldn't live with myself if I did.

You are not going to abandon your parent. You are reading this book because you want to care for your parent in the most loving way for everyone involved. Yours is a very difficult position to be in. Moving your parent in with you is a loving decision, but it is not the only loving decision; finding the best living arrangement for your parent is the goal. There are many possible paths. Your job is to find the correct one for you, your parent, and your family.

STATEMENT 5

> I know my mother thinks I don't care about her. That's not true, but she is always trying to make me feel bad.

You can't control what another person thinks. In most cases, you really don't know what is going on in another person's mind. Do you really know that your mother wants you to feel bad? Is your mother just trying to make you feel bad to manipulate a decision out of you? That may be true; but is it possible that because of your history with your parent you are just seeing hidden meanings in everything your parent says? Is it a combination? Only you know for sure.

If you are able to set aside the anxiety and fear over what was going on in your parent's mind, you will have an easier time with the move. You can't please everyone, but you can commit to doing the best you can.

Section III: Financial Motivation

Section III identifies whether you are making a decision to move your parent in based on financial pressure or financial motivation. Caring for an elderly parent with special health and emotional needs can be expensive, especially when insurance doesn't cover much of it. For many families, the financial aspect of caring for their parent is a strong motivator for moving him: "Dad makes too much money from social security and his pension to receive state aid, but doesn't make enough to live in an assisted-living facility. He can't live alone—what should we do?" If finances are a major factor in your decision, it is especially important that you approach the move with as much education as possible. Consider contacting an eldercare specialist, who can give you the details on state aid, Medicaid, and other resources.

If your motivation for making the move is based on financial gain, then you may be making a mistake that is more far reaching than just the challenges of caring for your aging parent.

If you scored an average of four or higher, you may be making a decision based on either faulty or limited information. Look at the resource section of this book and contact experts to see what financial help is available before you make your decision. In addition to actual financial help, there are many agencies that will assess your situation and find creative ways to meet your parent's needs as well as yours. An average score of three or less may indicate that although you may feel financial pressure, you are on your way to making a sound decision.

STATEMENT 1

Moving Dad in will be good for our family because he will help with our bills, and maybe even contribute to the addition we want to put on our house.

The advice from families who moved in an elderly parent for financial gain is usually a resounding, "Don't do it!" Any potential financial benefit was overshadowed by the consequences the unprepared family felt. Because their motivation was fueled by finances, they didn't always do their homework about the care their parent needed. They tended to gloss over the emotional impact and the financial cost that moving in another adult would have on their home life and family. There were many other areas of preparation, including caring for the elderly parent's emotional needs during the transition that were overlooked.

In addition, there was a level of guilt, especially if the arrangement wasn't working. What happens if your parent has a progressive disease such as Alzheimer's? What happens if your parent pays for an addition on your house, and then three years later his condition worsens? Families spoke of the difficulty they faced and extreme guilt they felt when moving their parent out after accepting money. In addition, if there is any chance your parent will require help from Medicaid it is possible Medicaid will require you to pay back any funds given to you by your parent over a specified numbers of years. To make sure this doesn't happen, speak with an eldercare lawyer or Medicaid specialist.

On the other hand, if after careful consideration, communication, and soul searching you have determined that you would like to move in a parent, and it so happens that he can help with the mortgage or even pay for the addition where he will live, that's different. Once again, the outcome appears the same, but the underlying motivation is different. You are moving the parent in to help them—not to profit from the decision. The financial assistance can be a by-product but should not be the impetus.

STATEMENT 2

> I don't trust my brother with Mom's money. If she lives here, we can at least oversee her finances and help her out.

If your parent is unable to oversee her own finances and you are concerned that another family member or even an unscrupulous salesperson will take advantage, you have options. If your primary concern and motivation is to protect your parent's finances, look in the resource section of this book before making a decision based on finances and find services that can help you set up financial trusts, powers of attorney, and other structures to protect your parent's assets. In addition, every state also has a government-run agency to protect seniors from abuse—financial and otherwise.

Once you have gathered information and know ways to protect your parent's assets, then you can contemplate moving her in with you. Then, and only then, can you be sure your motivation is not financially driven, but by the wish to care for your parent.

STATEMENT 3

We can't afford an assisted-living facility or home health care.

This may be true; however, before you jump to, "We have no choice because of our limited funds," contact some of the many agencies available that offer advice and guidance. You may be surprised at the many available avenues for caring for your parent. The AARP offers a wealth of information—look in the resource section of this book for their contact information. In addition, most states offer medical assistance for the elderly. You can also find less expensive day programs that could ease the financial burden of a personal home health aide. Do your homework, and then decide. You may find that after talking to the experts that you have options, but still want to move your parent in with you. That's great. Make an educated, willing decision rather than feeling backed into a corner; this assures a better outcome.

STATEMENT 4

I don't want Dad to use up all his money for a nurse or home health care.

Why not? What should he save his money for? An emergency? It is an emergency if he needs medical care and support that isn't covered by insurance. This doesn't mean you should waste or squander what money he has; however, using his available finances for whatever will best serve his emotional and physical health is money put to good use. Your dad may be hesitant about spending his money, saying he wants to save for the future—in this case, the future is now. Your job will be to help him relax so that he gets the care he needs today.

STATEMENT 5

Assisted-living facilities are a waste of money; they charge thousands—and for what?

Assisted-living facilities are expensive, that's a fact. On average, they cost anywhere from $2,800 to $5,500 per month. And in most cases, insurance does not cover any of the costs. However, if your parent is fortunate enough to be able to afford one, do not dismiss it until you weigh the pros and cons. Many elderly people have specific medical needs. In addition, they can suffer from depression when trying to adjust to losing their independence. They tend to feel less productive, capable, and much less mobile. In many cases, their social life also dwindles—isolation and loneliness is a significant problem. While few people jump at the chance to move into an assisted-living facility, many enjoy it once they have moved and are settled in.

The benefits include:
- Built-in social structure
- Independent living with an array of medical and social supports
- Meal services and community dining rooms so no one eats alone
- An on-site nutritionist creating food plans to optimize health, is especially helpful for those with diabetes, high blood pressure, allergies, high cholesterol, and other conditions that require special diets
- Activities such as lectures, book clubs, group exercise, game and card nights, movies, etc. are common offerings at most facilities
- Increased levels of care, as needed

- Shuttle services
- Twenty-four-hour a day emergency care
- Housekeeping and laundry services
- Basic medical care right on site, such as eye doctors, podiatrist, general practitioners, lab services for blood work, etc.
- Peace of mind for the family knowing that help is always minutes away
- Check-in services in many facilities; residents have a button to push each morning upon awakening, letting the staff know all is well
- Emergency call buttons in every bathroom

Some of the downsides include:
- Expense
- A la carte services—as needs increase the expenses increase as well
- Some assisted-living facilities prohibit kitchens in individual units—just refrigerators, microwaves, and hot plates—this can prove difficult for those who enjoy cooking for themselves
- Some facilities have restrictions regarding pets
- Planned menus and, for some, average quality of food
- Many facilities have small living units—300–900 square feet—the most reasonably priced units are studios or one bedroom
- Many facilities do not allow personal gardening, which can be a great loss; however, there may be communal gardening opportunities close by

It's a good idea to explore a variety of facilities before making any kind of decision. Look into locations where your parent knows someone already living there, even if it is a friend of a friend of a friend. A personal endorsement, even if it is from a distant acquaintance, goes a long way. Bring your parent; you may be pleasantly surprised at the variety of facility types you'll find, and there just might be something right for your parent. Once you've visited different locations, you can then make your decision from a fully educated perspective.

Section IV: Shaky Core-Family Foundation

Section IV identifies if you are making a decision to move in an aging parent to appease your partner or improve your marriage. Moving an elderly parent in to improve your marriage will be as effective as bringing a child into the world just to save your relationship. Although on rare occasions it does help, for the most part it leads to disaster. If you move a parent into a shaky core-family unit, you may be setting a domino effect in motion, which may ultimately tear your marital relationship apart.

If you scored an average of four or higher, you may be headed for a difficult time. Consider putting together a strong support network prior to making the move. An average of three or less may indicate that you have a solid relationship and core-family unit with the normal ups and downs that most families experience.

STATEMENT 1

If I take care of my mother-in-law, maybe my spouse will appreciate me.

Your spouse may appreciate your effort, but there is no guarantee. Before you take one step further in the process of moving in an elderly parent, you will need to separate three issues that are jumbled together in this statement:

1. What is best for your parent-in-law?
2. What is best for you and your family?
3. What effect will moving your parent-in-law into your home have on your already troubled relationship?

Partners who moved in a parent with the express purpose of eliciting a response from their spouse or who were trying to improve their marriage were disappointed across the board. Their own lives became more complicated, their relationships didn't improve, and they had less time alone with their partner. However, this is not to say that the move was always deemed unsuccessful. Many families in this circumstance felt the move was successful. The unsuccessful part was that their marital issues remained the same or worsened. Many expressed that having moved in their in-law diverted their attention away from their marriage and onto other issues, giving them a respite from their own problems. There are better ways to improve your marriage than moving in your spouse's parent. Read on and then decide what might be best for your parent-in-law, you and your family, and your marriage.

STATEMENT 2

My spouse made all the decisions and I am just going along with it. I won't rock the boat. Besides, this is what he/she wants. I'm just keeping my mouth shut.

The potential problem in this scenario is not that you are going along with what your spouse wants, but in how you choose to go along with what your spouse wants. There is no right or wrong in relationships, just what works for each person. There is no problem if you choose to allow your needs to take a back seat to your partner's; there is a problem if you make this decision and then resent it. This is especially true if you continually bring up your "generosity" while trying to coax appreciation or gratitude out of your spouse at every turn. If you are clear that your choice is to go along with your spouse's decision, then do so lovingly. If you think you can't do this, then this is the time to figure that out. Voice your opinion now, before your father-in-law moves in.

Those spouses who could not let go of the resentment fell into depression, anger, and stress over the move. Because they were unable to let go of the resentment, they ultimately took their frustration out on their partner, rather than looking at why they went along with the decision in the first place.

STATEMENT 3

It just seems as if it is happening around me.

Once again, you may have to make a decision to actively participate in the decision or lovingly step aside. Don't waste your energy feeling angry at yourself for what you did or didn't do—focus on the future. Moving an aging parent in with you is a life-changing decision. If you are feeling unhappy, overwhelmed, and out of control already, consider getting support for yourself.

STATEMENT 4

My marriage is so shaky; I could use the support and company.

Remember, your mother is moving in so that you can help her. It isn't that she won't be a comfort to you; however, her needs will be at the forefront. Consider getting the support from a therapist, clergy, or other family service organization prior to making a move that has potentially monumental consequences, both good and bad. Separate marital problems from the specific issue of moving an elderly parent into your home. They are separate—keep them that way. Remember, your marital problems may no longer be your focus once your parent moves in, but they will resurface with a vengeance when your parent is no longer in your home.

STATEMENT 5

> I can't talk to my spouse about how I feel about the move. He/she just gets angry and it causes too many problems.

Once again, moving in your parent will not resolve marital issues; in most cases it will make them worse. Consider getting marital help prior to deciding to move in your parent. If that is not an option, consider finding ways to get your own needs met while you are caring for the elderly parent. Look for services that offer support services for caregivers.

Section V: Impatience

Section V identifies whether you are rushing to make a decision based on arbitrary scheduling or the urgent pull to take care of business. The decision to move an elderly parent into your home means you will be removing (whether your parent goes willingly or not) a person not only from her home, but also from a lifestyle built over decades. It is a huge decision for everyone involved. A rushed decision can make the move harder for your parent because she will not have the time to mentally adjust. And it can potentially make it harder for you, as rushing through the process means it's less likely you will make a sound, educated, and well-thought-out decision.

If you scored an average of four or higher, you may be rushing to make a decision rather than taking time to make the right decision. An average of three or less may indicate that you have a healthy sense of urgency, but are decisive and ready to take action.

STATEMENT 1

We have to make the decision *right now*. What's there to talk about? Let's move Mom in and work out the details later. I can always call her doctor if there is a problem.

Imagine applying for a mortgage. You ask about the rates and terms of your loan. Your banker replies, "We'll start off with 7 percent, but we'll see what happens and adjust it as we go along." Would you really sign up for a mortgage without getting the details up front, especially with fairly big potential consequences? Probably not. The majority of families that made the decision to move in an elderly parent without first gathering information and planning and looking into the potential positives and negatives lamented, "If I had know this up front, I could have saved myself months of aggravation. If I knew what a difficult time Mom would have with the move, I might not have uprooted her so quickly."

Do yourself a favor—find out all you can up front. Talk to the doctors. Learn about the progression of any health issues. Find support systems. Find ways to respectfully transition your parent. You'll be happy you did.

STATEMENT 2

> After Dad moves in, if it doesn't work out, one of my siblings can take a turn.

That sounds great in theory. However, consider the move permanent; it could be emotionally distressing to your parent to be shuffled around. Your parent will have moved, stored, given away, and thrown away possessions. He is likely to want to settle in somewhere, to feel at home, to feel wanted. Do not consider the move a test run. If you need some sort of trial period, invite your parent for a long visit and make the permanent move once you are sure it is the right decision.

STATEMENT 3

> I've already scheduled the movers and arranged for storage. I don't want to disrupt the schedule.

The decision of whether or not to move your parent into your home is too important to rush based on an arbitrary schedule. The move itself has to take precedence over everything else. Your parent is giving up her previous lifestyle—and so are you. It may be better to rearrange the schedule and focus on making the right decision rather than honor a random moving date for convenience sake.

STATEMENT 4

> If we don't do this now, we'll have to pay for a nurse to come in and look in on Mom.

It is better to spend time and money up-front than make a mistake or miss out on important fact-finding time. Only you know your financial constraints; however, if your parent needs a nurse during the time it takes you to decide whether or not to move her into your house or another facility, or even to prepare your house for maximum safety, you need to find a way to make this happen. Don't rush the move or the necessary preparation to make the move safe and successful.

STATEMENT 5

> I want to handle all this before we go away on vacation (or start a new job, have a baby, and so on).

Once again, this decision is too important to rush based on a schedule. It may be better to rearrange the schedule or wait until you come back from vacation or after you've started your new job than rush your family before they are ready. It may take your parent some time to get used to the idea of moving. Within reason, give him the time he needs to adjust and emotionally prepare for the total change in lifestyle. A relaxed move will make for a more relaxed transition into the new living arrangement.

Section VI: Adult-Child Stance

Section VI identifies if you are making a decision from the adult-child perspective rather than the independent-adult mindset. If you had a difficult childhood, were raised by strong-willed or self-centered parents, or feel unhealed from your past, it can be difficult, even as an adult, to break free from parental control. Adults still trapped in the child role will have to be careful when making the decision to have a parent move in. In many cases, their decision will be laden with ulterior motives: to gain acceptance or approval, alleviate guilt, to prove one's worth, or worse . . . to punish. Base the decision on wanting to care for your parent. Seeking approval and trying to heal unresolved issues will not lead you to the best or healthiest decision for you or your parent.

If you scored an average of three or higher, you may be setting yourself up for disappointment by trying to heal your relationship with your parent by moving her into your home or making the decision out of a feeling of pressure from your parent. An average of two or less may indicate you can see your parent for her strengths and weaknesses, have forgiven mistakes, and ultimately see your parent from an adult perspective rather than through the eyes of the wounded child.

STATEMENT 1

This is my home and family with my rules; he'll be a guest here. I hope he will be able to respect that.

Once you move your parent into your home, he is no longer a guest; he is a member of your household. If you outline the rules that each family member follows, then everyone will most likely respect the rules. Do not expect anyone to read your mind or just intuitively know what you want—work as a team and create guidelines. This will make the transition easier for everyone. Respect trickles down from a kind and compassionate leader of the household, not from a tyrant. (See Chapter 4 for guidelines on setting family rules.)

STATEMENT 2

I'll show through example how parenting should be done. He'll have to respect me when he sees me raising my own kids.

We all make mistakes. Caring for your parent can be an opportunity to see your parent as human, with good and bad qualities. It is also an opportunity to forgive and move past old hurts. Families who are able to keep an open, loving heart have the best outcomes when it came to moving in an elderly parent. Expressing kindness and love has a greater impact than actions with the intention of, "I'll show them." Also, a parent who is profoundly self-centered or narcissistic would never be able to learn a lesson through example. He would never see himself as needing to learn and, most likely, would see your good parenting as proof of their good job raising you.

STATEMENT 3

Considering what a bad mother she was, she should be grateful that I am willing to take care of her. If she's not, we'll just have to move her out.

The families we talked to who could not take care of their elderly parent from a loving heart caused emotional distress for themselves, their children, and their parents. Do your best to let go of anger, resentment, and the need to punish your mother for who she was and who she wasn't. If you can't, maybe the move is not the best for you or your family. In addition, it is never a good idea to half commit to a move. Once you move her in, she is probably staying for life, or until you find her health requires a different living arrangement. Never underestimate how difficult it will be to move your parent out once you have moved her in.

STATEMENT 4

This will give me and Dad a chance to repair our relationship. Besides, I'm sure he'll mellow with age.

Living with your parent may give you an opportunity to repair your relationship with him. However, it won't just magically happen; you will have to work on it. In addition, your parent won't turn into a different kind of person. While it is true many people mellow with age, it is equally true that people become more themselves as they grow older. For example, the father who had a violent temper in his prime may be a little less volatile, but may be more judgmental and harsh now. A woman who tended to let her husband make all of the decisions during their marriage may ultimately rebel and want to take charge of her life as she ages; however, it is equally possible that she becomes more dependent on her children.

Don't count on your parent's personality changing just because of the new living arrangement. If your parent was a stickler for tidiness and order, don't expect that to change just because he is living under your roof. If your relationship was difficult when you were growing up, it may still be. The advantage now is that you are an adult and no longer need your parent to be a certain way; you don't need to be taken care of. You will have a better chance of making the move successful if you are able to see your parent from the adult perspective, not the child's viewpoint.

STATEMENT 5

Dad expects me to take care of him. What else can I do? I don't have much choice.

You have many choices. Reread the guilt section of The Moving-In Quiz. You will do what is best for you, your family, and your parent. You are the adult and have the right to make decisions about your own life. Moving in an elderly parent is not the only loving decision when it comes to care. Look at the available resources and your options. Regardless of what your parent expects or thinks, you do have choices. Just because someone else has an expectation of you doesn't mean that you must fulfill that expectation. One of the gifts of being an adult is that you have the right to choose how you live your life and react to the consequences of those choices. Choose what is best for you and your family.

Overall Score

Add your total numbers from each section and divide by seven. That is your overall score. If you scored an average of three or under, you are probably on the right track to making a good decision for you, your parent, and your family. You can probably make the move successfully. You have most likely educated yourself on your parent's condition, and are available to look at potential issues and problems as they arise. Your overall underlying motivation is to care for your parent in the best way possible.

If you scored an average of four or five, then you are potentially heading down a difficult path when considering the move. You may need to do a little more research on your parent's condition. You may need to look into what can happen once your parent has moved in with you. Are you rushing the decision? Check the individual sections where you scored high. Don't be hasty; make the best decision possible for everyone concerned.

You are likely to have a successful move if you:

- Have realistic expectations about the work involved in caring for an elderly parent
- Do homework concerning your parent's condition
- Have a strong core-family relationship

- Are able to welcome your parent into your home as a member of the household
- Are flexible
- Are open to talking about issues as they arise
- Create guidelines and are in agreement prior to the move
- Forgive mistakes (your own and other people's)
- Have a strong and healthy motivation to care for your parent
- Have resources and support for the specific medical and emotional conditions of your parent
- Continue to carve out time to spend alone with your spouse/partner/core family

Your move may be more challenging if you:

- Have an uncommunicative or tumultuous spousal relationship
- Rush the decision
- Make the decision thinking it would be short-term
- Do little, if any, research on your parent's medical condition
- Have ulterior motives other than caring for your parent
- Have a difficult time with acceptance and hold onto the past
- See your parent as a guest in your home rather than a member of the family
- Have misconceptions about what the move will mean
- Make the decision under duress or to please your spouse

Additional Food for Thought: Life Cycles

While not a part of The Moving-In Quiz, there are additional factors to consider when deciding to move your parent in. Answer the following questions as best you can, and then read on for analysis of your answers.

LIFE CYCLES

How often do the following apply?

1 Never **2** Almost Never **3** Sometimes **4** Almost Always **5** Always

___	My parents took care of their parents. I want to take care of mine. This is the family cycle that feels right, and I am happy to do it.
___	I love my Dad, and I think it will enhance this part of his life to be with us. And it will be wonderful for our children to know their grandfather.
___	It gives us great joy to care for my father as he cared for us when we were kids.
___	It feels right to have three generations living in the house.
___	Aging is part of life. This is what I would want when I am older, so I want to give that to my parent. I know this may not be easy, but I am willing to do what it takes to make the move work.

Total: ___ / 5 = ___

Life Cycles

Separate from The Moving-In Quiz, the above set of questions is intended to clarify your own perspectives on family, aging, and life-cycle issues. There are no individual cautions here; rather, think of each question as an opportunity to discuss and identify your own feelings. If you scored an average of four or higher, you may be making a decision based on the thought, "We *should* move our parents into our home" rather than a heartfelt yearning to do so. Take a look at your motives and then decide. An average of three or less may indicate that you are truly of the mindset that a family sticks together and each member is responsible for nurturing and caring its members.

Lessons Learned

Hopefully, by now you have uncovered any hidden agendas, ulterior motives, misconceptions, or blind spots you may have. Armed with this information, you can start thinking about what is right for everyone involved. Read through the rest of the chapters and see what other families encountered when they actually moved an elderly parent in with them. Look at the facts and then make your final decision.

However, if you are like most people, you have already made your decision and are just looking for evidence to support it. That's okay, too. *When Your Parent Moves In* will shed light on what can happen, what challenges you may face, and potential management of issues as they arise. The better educated and prepared you are the better chance you have for making the move work. And, if you decide that the move isn't right for you, you will have resources to make other loving decisions and can feel good about your choice, knowing it is probably the best decision for all concerned.

chapter 3

expect the unexpected

IT'S TUESDAY AFTERNOON. You arrive home to find the front door wide open and nobody home. Or, you walk into the laundry room and the iron has been on all night or a bottle of heart medication, with no childproof cap, is sitting next to the giant cookie bag. You are about to leave the house for your much-needed haircut, and just as you are about to go your mother decides at that precise moment she desperately needs your help or seems incredibly anxious and doesn't want you to leave. Or worse, your father, who resists using his cane, trips and falls and needs emergency medical care.

ONE FAMILY'S EXPERIENCE *Vicky and Sam*

I had a long day, and I couldn't wait to get home. As soon as I walked in the door, I see both my dad and his old grey-haired beagle stretched out on the sofa, sleeping like babies. I couldn't help but smile. However, within seconds of walking in the front door, I smelled something burning. I ran into the

53

kitchen and saw a pot of burnt soup on the lit gas-burning stove. "Dad," I screamed, "You left the stove on again!"

He woke up from a sound sleep and felt terrible that he not only left the stove on, but also that he upset me. "Why can't you be more careful? Do you want to burn the house down?" I know he is forgetful, but it was getting to be too much. I lost it, and really started to yell. What could have been simply bad, I made worse.

Just when you feel you are getting a handle on living with your parent, circumstances change. You can't predict the unpredictable; however, you can identify some common causes for the unplanned events that happen when you move your parent in with you. This knowledge will lessen the shock to your system when the unexpected happens. The following are the most common causes of unpredictable disruptions to family routines:

- Forgetfulness
- Anxiety and frustration
- Inappropriate behavior
- Stubbornness
- Illness
- Unsure how to act
- Change in priorities
- The "Why did you do that?" factor

Forgetfulness

Many families who have chosen to move a parent in with them did so out of concern for their parent's failing memory.

Forgetfulness can be distressing to witness: your mother forgets to take her medicine; your father forgets to pay his bills; or your uncle forgets where he lives. However, not all memory loss should raise the red flag. To begin with, not all memory loss is a sign of dementia, and not all dementia is a sign of Alzheimer's disease. There are different types of memory impairment, some of which are a normal part of the aging process. Some are not; your job as caretaker will be to determine if your parent's memory loss is normal (then your next course of action will be to create workarounds) or not (then you will need to take your parent to the doctor).

Causes of Memory Loss

There are many causes of memory loss. Did you know that some of your daily decisions affect memory, and some decisions made thirty, forty, or even fifty years ago may have an effect today? For example, do you remember when you were in your twenties, joking with your friends after a night of bar hopping that the evening's activities may have cost you more than a few brain cells? That was accurate. You start losing brain cells, in a minimal way, beginning in your twenties. According to Harvard Health Publications, excessive drinking (having more than two drinks a day) significantly increases your risk factor for dementia. Your morning hangover may have been the immediate result of your late night out; however, the long-term results of repeated nights on the town may be diminished memory as you age.

Brain cells die over time; that's normal. The loss will probably have little impact on your life until you reach your mid forties. At that point, you may begin to notice a change. Have you ever walked into a room and not been able to remember why you went there in the first place? How about running into an old friend that you've known for years, but now you can't, for the life of you, remember his name? What about looking for your eye glasses only to find them sitting on top of your head? It happens to all of us, especially as we approach fifty. The progression of memory loss is even more rapid at your parent's age. These types of memory interruptions are frustrating, and they are also normal.

You and your parent are in the same boat, along with countless other people in their forties, fifties, sixties, and beyond. This type of memory loss is recent-memory loss. Your ability to retrieve or access immediate information slows, but doesn't stop. Recent-memory loss also interferes with your ability to effectively put thoughts in a queue.

For example, you are at the Home Depot speaking with someone in the kitchen appliance department. The salesperson is describing the features of a refrigerator you are interested in buying. As he is speaking, you think of several questions. You politely listen to him and wait for him to complete his pitch before you ask your questions. However, after he completes his speech, two minutes later, you have no idea what you wanted to ask. Five minutes later, when you have continued shopping, those questions pop back into your mind. Your short-term and long-term memory are still intact; your mind is still functioning properly, but because of the slow down you may have a difficult time remembering recent thoughts or conversations. It may be normal, but it is still frustrating.

Rest assured that the word you are looking for will eventually come to mind. You will find your eye glasses. You will remember what you needed in the guest room, and you will remember what you wanted to say. This is the same for your parent. Although this type of absentmindedness is normal, it can still create chaos. If your mother is making tea and walks into the living room while waiting for the water to boil, it is very possible that she will get distracted and forget the pot is on the stove. Maybe it is time to get a whistling teapot.

According to Harvard Health Publications, the factors contributing to memory loss include:

- High blood pressure
- High levels of LDL (bad) cholesterol
- Low levels of HDL (good) cholesterol
- Excessive alcohol, tobacco, and/or drug use
- Stroke
- Head injury
- Depression

So What Can I Do?

While depression among the elderly is not uncommon (late-life depression affects more than 6 million Americans), don't assume that if your parent is depressed it will right itself: "My mom was always upbeat—I'm sure this will pass." This may not be true anymore. You may need to address this depression with her physician to come up with some ways to help her feel better.

If your parent falls into the group experiencing normal age-related memory loss (not caused by depression), there are several things you can do to help.

- *Use brain power.* Give your parent crossword puzzles or other word or math games. Encourage your parent to read, take a class, or learn to draw. Focused mental activity has been proven to help stimulate brain-cell growth as well as slow down the deterioration process.

- *Reduce or eliminate tobacco and alcohol use.* Both are shown to double the risk of dementia.
- *Get moving.* Exercise has been proven to create more blood vessels as well as nerve cells to the brain. It also reduces depression.
- *Eat healthier.* A healthier diet lowers bad cholesterol and raises good cholesterol, which improves memory and overall brain function.

If your dad is becoming frustrated by his memory loss, in addition to making an appointment with the doctor, consider helping him with the following:

- *Make lists.* Create a list of things you would like your dad to be aware of each day. This way he doesn't have to rely on memory. Leave them in sensible places around the house. Many families we talked to found it helpful to their parent to leave lists of just about everything from how to use the iron, where to find knitting yarn, important phone numbers, when to feed the dog, and how to use the washing machine. You can give your parent a greater sense of autonomy if you can create this how-to so your parent doesn't have to ask for help, or worse, give up on certain tasks.
- *Create routines.* If you create a schedule and stick to it, he will have an easier time remembering those events. Keep in mind that normal aging memory loss does not affect long-term memory.
- *Recite a daily recap of events.* It will help him store and retrieve the information more easily. Remember, long-term memory is probably fine.

- *Keep items in the same place.* Have a place for keys, eye glasses, remote control, phone books, and so on. This cuts down on the confusion.

If your parent's absentmindedness is causing health risks, such as leaving the stove on, then you may be forced to make the stove (or iron, if that is left on) off limits. Your parent may be relegated to the microwave and wrinkly shirts. You may have to make an argument for household safety.

Normal Memory Loss Versus Serious Impairment

The previous paragraphs discuss the normal aging process as it relates to memory slow down. There are, however, more serious types of memory loss. How can you tell if your parent's forgetfulness has gone beyond the normal aging process? Carefully think about your parent's condition and answer the following:

- Is my parent's memory loss affecting her ability to perform basic self-care tasks?
- Has my parent forgotten how to perform tasks (such as cook, pay bills, do laundry) that she used to know how to do?
- Does my parent have a difficult time learning new things?
- Does my parent repeat herself within one conversation?

See Chapter 5 for a more detailed assessment. However, if you answered yes to any of the questions above, this may be a sign that your parent is experiencing more than just normal memory loss. If that is the case, then simple off-limit rules will not work. You will need to arrange a medical assessment, and it may ultimately mean that your parent needs constant supervision, especially in the case of Alzheimer's or other mentally degenerative diseases where safety is an issue. Don't fall into the trap of ignoring obvious signs of a problem. It is easy to say, "I forget things all the time—Dad is just fine." Go through the assessments and let trained professionals determine the level of severity. If other family members are noticing a problem in your parent, maybe you should listen.

Once you are aware of the type of forgetfulness typical of your parent, you will no longer be surprised when it happens. You may be annoyed, but not surprised. Once you are aware how forgetfulness typically manifests, you can create ways to work around it. Use the previous lists as a starting point for your own thinking process.

Also, think about the effectiveness of the reminders you give your parent now. Does, "Don't forget to unplug the iron when you are done" work? Probably not. Your mom knows to unplug the iron; she just forgets. Maybe the solution is no ironing during the day. This may require you to put the ironing board away and out of sight. Or you may find that leaving a checklist by the ironing board works just fine. Most importantly, try not to get angry—it isn't your mother's fault. Understanding the causes of forgetfulness may not eliminate your frustration, but more knowledge and compassion will make for a more peaceful home.

Anxiety and Frustration

Anxiety and frustration are common emotions for seniors who are taken out of familiar surroundings and routines. It is especially frightening for those who are aware that they are less capable. Diabetes sufferers can experience severe emotional distress if their vision begins to fail. Alzheimer patients in mid stage of the disease often experience a great deal of fear when left alone. They are aware enough to know that they aren't what they used to be, but not clear enough to take control of their lives.

Once your father feels dependent on you, his anxiety and neediness may increase when you are unavailable. In addition, his frustration over his physical condition, over which he has no control, can enrage him. If possible, help him feel independent by allowing him to perform the tasks that he can. Allow him to maintain a familiar routine for as long as possible. If he went to the barber the first Tuesday of every month, help him keep that appointment. If he played cards with his friends on Monday nights, help him maintain that connection.

Be patient with your parent's anxiety, and help to assuage fears by warning him before you leave the house—don't just announce it as you are walking out the door. A simple, "Dad, I am leaving in half an hour, is there anything you need before I go?" will be helpful for all of you. Consider telling him what time you plan to return.

Most important, after you make the announcement, make sure you do leave in that timeframe. When people feel needy, they can be manipulative. If your father knows that when you say you are leaving in half an hour you mean it, he will be less likely to bring up last-minute emergencies. You must create and maintain reliable and dependable boundaries; it does not help your parent if you don't stand by your word. When confronted with a minor problem minutes before your well-presented exit, your job is to say, "I am returning in one hour. I'll take care of it then."

If your parent is truly anxious when left alone, consider asking a family member to stay in the house while you are away. If that is not possible, find out if a local volunteer group or home health aide service can send someone to your house for a few hours a day. It may not be ideal, but keep in mind that everyone's safety, physical and emotional, is paramount. See the reference section for resources on home health care.

Inappropriate Behavior

Many families joke about cringe-inducing conversations their live-in parent initiated during a holiday party or Thanksgiving dinner. Socially inappropriate behavior or conversation can create embarrassment for every member of the family. And once it starts, it probably won't stop. Here are three of the most common reasons why:

- *Loss of impulse control.* As we age, most of us will feel less of a need to conform; we feel we have earned the right to speak up and say what we feel. This, coupled with our dying brain cells, decreases our ability to quickly censor ourselves. Therefore, we may speak first and think later. Or speak first and forget we said anything at all. It isn't harmful to your parent—just embarrassing to you.
- *What you find interesting changes.* People like to talk about important issues in their lives. If your parent's activities are focused on her doctor appointments and

medical issues, that will most likely be the focus of her conversations. Much to your dismay, it is only natural that she will want to share personal medical issues, even at parties and family dinners.

- *Less need for social niceties.* Because of illness or circumstance, your mother may be taking herself out of the social fabric of society. She is still part of your household, but might feel separate. One of the side effects of isolation is that those social niceties become less important. Another reason for the decrease in social etiquette is fear. If your mother is growing weaker and feeling vulnerable and insecure, her survival mechanism may be kicking in. She will do whatever it takes to survive. Her behavior may seem more pushy or aggressive, or even angry. This may be because she wants something she feels she can't get or do on her own, and is afraid if she doesn't push it won't happen. If you remind yourself of why your parent is acting the way she is, you will have an easier time not only accepting her behavior but also helping alleviate some of her fears that are causing it.

Stubbornness

Most people will rebel, on some level, if they feel that they are either being pressured to conform or someone is trying to interfere with their decision making or personal sense of freedom. Think back over what has happened between you and your parent over the last year. Maybe you noticed your dad was less capable of self-care and stepped in to help. Just because your dad needed help, doesn't mean that he wanted help or was able accept or appreciate it. Did you pressure your father to sell his home and move into your house? Does he feel pushed around? Out of control? Any of these feelings, whether real or imagined, could create a need to rebel in most people.

Rebellion can surface with a lot of force. Maybe your parent isn't angry with you at all, just with his illness or condition. If you feel your dad is acting difficult, purposely disruptive, or completely rejecting of help you may need to have an exploratory dialogue and find out what he is feeling. Maybe he needs to discuss the difficulty of the situation. (See Chapter 9 for more details.) Consider starting gently with, "You seem aggravated. Would you like to talk about what is going on?" Avoid hurtful accusations such as, "You are acting like a spoiled child." Always start by noticing feelings. It is less confrontational and more supportive. Don't make the conversation about you: "You are making my life miserable."

Also, consider letting your parent offer solutions. For example, "You seem so angry all the time. Have you thought about ways that we can make this better?" Or, "I have some thoughts. Would you like to hear them?" Rebellion can be a sign that your parent didn't feel that he participated in the decision to move in with you or is frustrated or doesn't like to be told what to do or doesn't agree with his diagnosis or is depressed or a combination of these or other factors. Rebellion is a sign of unrest, and the first step is to discuss it.

Many families who described their live-in parent as a bad child eventually improved the situation by restoring some sense of autonomy to their parent. For example, one daughter went out of her way to avoid saying no all of the time. Her mother was constantly talking about a trip she wanted to take. As a dutiful daughter, she would gently remind her mother that she needed dialysis and the trip was impractical. It dawned on her one day that maybe her mother was fantasizing or just wanted to think about her own life the way she wanted to. The next time her mother brought up the trip, the daughter said, "That would be an amazing trip." Her mother relaxed, she relaxed, and they went about their day a little more peacefully.

Illness

If a parent has moved in with you, chances are the impetus for the move was health. Once your parent moves in, you become responsible. If your mom gets sick while living under your roof, you will be the one she turns to. Keep in mind that the saying "when it rains it pours" is never truer than when it comes to health and the elderly. One illness may set off a chain reaction. Be proactive: Make sure mom has her medication and takes it; make sure it never runs out by keeping up with reorders; make sure she makes her doctor appointments; keep up with physicals.

Most important, if your parent has a disease or progressive condition, find out everything you can about it. Learn what can come next. (See Chapter 4 for more details.) You don't want to get caught off guard. However, it doesn't mean you won't, even with this type of preparation. Just because you know your mom has Alzheimer's and, that most patients in mid to late stage express aggression and even combative behavior, doesn't mean you will be truly prepared for it when it happens. However, if you are aware of the potential symptoms, you will at least know what to do when it does happen.

Unsure How to Act

Most people settle into an environment more easily when they know what is expected of them and how the family usually operates. The perfect time to set ground rules for the new living arrangement is when it is still hypothetical and not an active, emotionally charged situation. Setting the ground rules ahead of time makes it easier to give gentle reminders such as, "Remember, head phones on the television after 10:00 P.M. because Billy needs quiet in order to fall asleep," as opposed to, "Dad! Your TV is too loud and you are keeping us awake." How was Grandpa supposed to know unless you told him?

You don't like to be told what to do. Neither does your parent. Therefore, rather than giving your parent a list of requirements, sit down as a family and have an open discussion. Try to make the conversation fun—a way to start thinking about your new life together.

Let Grandpa contribute to the list. Maybe he is a stickler for a neat laundry room. Let him create a rule, "No clean clothes are to be left in the dryer. Clothes must be taken out, folded, and brought upstairs when they are done." Maybe you like to sleep late on Sundays. You can make a rule that says, "No guests at the house on Sunday before noon." Talking about the rules will help you, as the parent of the house, decide which rules will help keep your home a peaceful place.

Many families who have moved their elderly parent into their homes regret not spelling out the rules upfront in addition to agreeing to follow them. Many waited until a situation arose and then were faced with having a difficult and sometimes confrontational conversation. Create family rules as a unit, but keep them simple and few. Going overboard will just create confusion and resentment.

Here are some examples of things you should decide on ahead of time:

- Where medication goes
- What the pets eat
- Whether or not the dog is allowed on the sofa
- Who helps with dishes
- When the house needs to quiet down to prepare for sleep
- Who contributes what to the household (see Chapter 5 for more details)
- When dinner is
- Where the cars should be parked
- What language is inappropriate in front of the kids
- Where people can smoke
- Whether or not alcohol is permitted in the house
- If cookies and snacks are okay for the kids and in what circumstance (maybe no junk food in the kitchen where the kids can find it, but feel free to hide it in the pantry)
- When core-family alone time is
- The bathroom schedule (if there's sharing, a schedule is crucial)

This list should get you thinking about what types of routines will cut down on the unexpected upsets to the harmony of the house. See Chapter 10 for more information on preserving family harmony.

Change in Priorities

When your life is active and your schedule feels out of control, it is no surprise that you will run late from time to time.

When your life is less scheduled, as your mother's probably is, she may have been looking forward to going shopping with you as you promised. If you told your mom you would take her on Saturday at 11:00, she is most likely ready at 10:30, and has been looking forward to it all week. Saturday rolls around and you are not ready because you've been getting the kids ready for soccer. She wants to go at 11:00 as planned. While you understand that schedules change and plans are disrupted, your parent may have a difficult time with that and create unexpected problems around the change. Know that the trip to the store may be more important to her than you can understand. Let her know as soon as you know that the plans have changed and give her a firm time when you can take her. Stick to the new schedule as best as you can. She may hold onto her grudge all day. Acknowledge her upset feelings, explain what happened, apologize, and then move on.

The "Why Did You Do That?" Factor

The "Why did you do that" factor is when you want to say to your parent, "Why did you think it was okay for you to climb up on the chair to change the light bulb? You are still in a cast." Or, "Why did you forget to close the front door when you left the house?" The list of why's will go on and on. These, you will probably have to live with. In many cases, the "Why did you do that" behavior happens because of forgetfulness or out of denial that he has limitations. Encourage your parent to do the things he can do independently and safely as well as gently reminding him that you are there to help.

Lessons Learned

You can't plan for everything. However, you can adapt and handle what comes your way if you remember the most important word to live by: forgiveness. Agree to treat your parent as an adult, not as a bad child: "We're not mad at you; we're upset with the situation. Everyone makes mistakes."

There are no permanent fixes or solutions. As you read through the remainder of this book, you will identify methods to help create and maintain balance within your newly expanded living arrangement. Be open to the solutions offered and to creating your own solutions that will be best for your family.

chapter 4

setting the stage for success

LIKE EVERYTHING ELSE in life, when it comes to caring for an aging parent there is no such thing as perfection. There is no way to be the perfect caregiver. There is no way to permanently solve your parent's problems. There is no way to continually keep a loving, open heart free from pain when you are the caregiver. It is difficult to watch your parent grow weaker and realize you don't have all the time in the world. Just as you seem to understand your parent's needs and have finally developed a good routine, life changes. Needs change. Your family changes. This change can be upsetting, too. Doing the best you can is all you can realistically demand of yourself.

You can, however, increase your odds of caring for your parent successfully if you are prepared. Preparation entails learning everything you can about your parent's medical condition. When you make the decision to move your parent in, don't just look at the impact the decision will have on you and your family today, but what tomorrow may bring as well. Unfortunately for Rachel and Jim, they didn't prepare, and this is what happened to them.

ONE FAMILY'S EXPERIENCE *Rachel and Jim*

Twenty-twenty hindsight isn't worth much. However, if four years ago someone told me that moving my mother-in-law in would change my life—and not for the better—that would have been information worth paying for. Rachel and I married right out of college and just celebrated our twenty-sixth wedding anniversary. We've got two great kids, one married and the other just finishing up college. No grandkids yet, but we're hoping. About four years ago, Rachel noticed that her mom, Sarah, was behaving erratically. When we tried to talk to her about it, she became irate and couldn't fathom what we were talking about.

Sarah was eighty-four years old and forgetful, agitated, and often unreasonable. But recently, her behavior seemed to be getting more extreme. Rachel took her mom to a series of doctors to see if she was okay. She wasn't—Sarah had Alzheimer's disease. We were upset, but didn't know the extent of what the diagnosis meant.

That night, Rachel opened a discussion, or rather a monologue, laying out all possible scenarios for her mother's care. It ended with, "Mom should move in with us and we could look out for her. And you know what? It will be fine. Mom's got money, so maybe she can help put an addition on our house and live in that. I think that might be the best solution. That way she could move in, still have her own space, and we could keep an eye on her. So, Jim, let's move Mom in with us. What do you think?" Within an hour, Rachel was on the phone telling her mother that she should move in.

I had my reservations, but didn't say much. I was somewhat surprised at Rachel's decision, only because she and her mom hadn't always gotten along. Rachel had a hard time with

Sarah's critical nature; but, if that's what she wanted . . . I also thought the addition on the house was a good idea and said so.

Now, four years later, Sarah's condition has worsened. Her temper is out of control. She rages and blames, has bouts of violence and denial, and if we don't watch her every minute she wanders, lost, around the neighborhood. We are worried for her safety and our sanity. It's devastating to witness Sarah's deterioration and Rachel's guilt for feeling ill equipped to take care of her mother.

When I bring up moving Mom into a place where she can get better care, I hear, "You can take her money, but you can't take care of her." I am trapped by the financial decision to accept money for the addition on the house, the emotional decision of avoiding a real conversation up front, and am caught between what my wife wants and what I think is right. Worse, Rachel is so frozen with guilt that she can't make a decision at all.

There is no end in sight—just frustration. I hate walking into my own house. I never know if Sarah will be having a good or bad day. Even after Sarah passes away (and of course I feel guilty for thinking in those terms), there may still be years of fallout in my marriage. In the quiet of my own thoughts, the truth is . . . moving my mother-in-law in with us was the worst decision (or nondecision) of my life.

Jim and Rachel are in a tough position. Sarah has Alzheimer's disease and is on a steady decline. Their lives are in turmoil; they are exhausted and on the brink of divorce. If they had taken The Moving-In Quiz from Chapter 2, they most likely would have scored high in six out of the seven categories, indicating potential warning signs for the move.

Jim and Rachel made some big mistakes. However, moving Sarah in wasn't necessarily one of them; but moving her in without researching her illness, discussing the potential impact it may have on the family, and preparing for the inevitable progression of the disease were all major oversights with devastating consequences. Education, communication, and preparation would have dramatically increased Jim, Rachel, and Sarah's chances of a better outcome. This is especially true when taking care of a family member with a progressive disease such as Alzheimer's.

Alzheimer's disease is the most common form of dementia, with over 5 million Americans afflicted. Unlike some of the other forms of dementia where the symptoms are treatable and even curable, Alzheimer's is a noncurable, progressive brain disease that is marked by stages ranging from normal functioning to severe or late stage, when the afflicted may be unable to walk, speak, smile, swallow, or control normal body functions. It is a tragic disease that devastates the entire family.

If your parent is diagnosed with Alzheimer's disease or some other progressive illness, you must do your homework and know exactly what's in store before you make your next move. It is common to move a parent in who is showing moderate symptoms only to have their condition sharply decline a year or two later. The decline can include anger, unpredictable behavior, wandering, incontinence, hallucinations, refusal to eat, blaming, and outbursts. You may not need help with care at first, but many families find that as the disease progresses they ultimately need additional assistance from an experienced medical professional. The decision to move your parent in may be a good one; however, you must take the future into account when making your decision.

Gather Information

Lack of information may lead you to underplay your parent's condition and ultimate prognosis. This could lead to a difficult situation where you find yourself scrambling to hire experienced home health care. You may be in a position where you have to move your parent out of your home and into a more intensive-care facility; this brings a new set of stresses for you and your parent, especially if you haven't researched appropriate care facilities. Research your parent's condition and ultimate prognosis. Then, take the time to find:

- The right agencies for home health care
- What types of care are covered by your insurance
- Any assisted-living facilities that specialize in care for the type of illness your parent has

Information will not only prepare you for the future, but will also alleviate much of the guilt you experience if you ultimately feel unable to care for you parent, because you will have had a chance to speak to experts and other families who are in the same boat.

When you understand your parent's condition and his medical needs, you will be more equipped to make an informed decision as to whether or not you can safely and effectively care for your parent. An informed decision is always best.

Open the Lines of Communication

As soon as you have a diagnosis, initiate two groups of conversations. The first series of conversations are with experts in the field. Once you learn how your parent's symptoms may present, in what time frame, and the best ways to manage them, you are ready for the second set of conversations. Speak with family members who will be affected by your parent's illness. This includes spouses, siblings, children, and so on. Don't make unilateral decisions, and let everyone express their concerns. Make sure everyone knows what the upcoming years and months will bring regarding your parent's care. You will want your siblings to know what you are faced with. You will want your spouse and children to know what their lives may look like when symptoms progress.

You can't plan for everything, but you can be prepared. Denial will only make life worse when the reality presents itself. Preparation takes time; it requires research and setting up resources for the future as life continues to change. Preparation is both tangible (safety proofing the house before an elderly person moves in) and intangible (emotionally readying for the change in lifestyle).

Regarding emotions surrounding a parent's move, in the case of Jim and Rachel, Jim was never particularly fond of Sarah's temper, or disposition for that matter. There was no reason to think that those traits would change once she moved into the house. Jim and Rachel should have discussed how Sarah's personality and her mental deterioration could affect the family dynamic and harmony. As it turned out, Sarah's temper and unpredictable behavior (exaggerated by the disease) were unbearable for Jim and Rachel. In addition, Sarah was a tough mom—always critical. Rachel had a difficult time throughout her life with Sarah's negativity, and it didn't get any easier once she moved in.

In addition, even though your parent may be ill, still include her (as much as possible) in the conversation about her future. Jim and Rachel left Sarah out of the loop—that just made Sarah angrier. Throughout Sarah's life she was strong, independent, and stubborn. At eighty-four, she was still that way. It was a mistake for Rachel to come in and take over, barely giving her mom time to wrap her mind around the idea, let alone participate in the decision.

Rachel's domination added to Sarah's frustration—she had no control. While it was true Sarah couldn't be left alone and the final decision was not hers to make, she would have liked to be part of the decision-making conversation. Because she wasn't included, Sarah built up her own feelings of resentment rather than recognizing that her daughter and son-in-law wanted to help. It is possible that Sarah would never have moved peacefully or remembered that she agreed to the move, but in the moment, discussion and sensitivity to her needs would have given Sarah a feeling of control over her own life, which was rapidly spinning out of control.

What Happened with Jim, Rachel, and Sarah?

Predictably and sadly, over the next year Sarah's Alzheimer's progressed. She was forgetful and would endanger herself by wandering around the neighborhood and having fits of temper and abusive behavior that were frightening to witness.

Rachel wanted to care for her mother at all costs. Her guilt kept her from seeing what was actually best for Sarah. Rachel stubbornly held on to the notion of what she should be able to do. Rachel was overwhelmed by the situation and by her mother's behavior. She continued to take her own frustrations out on the only person around for her—Jim. This just added to her own guilty feelings as she pushed him away.

Ultimately, Rachel and Jim realized they needed help. So they hired a home health care worker to come to the house during the day when they were out, as well as to help at night getting Sarah ready for bed. The aide was helpful in many ways. Not only did she help with Sarah, she also gave Rachel and Jim reading material and told them about support sites online so they could talk to others in similar situations and understand they weren't failing Sarah.

Having the home health aide changed the dynamic in Rachel and Jim's home. Now, there was another person dedicated to Sarah's care, giving Jim and Rachel a needed break as well as the opportunity to spend more time together. Because they were able to unwind, just a little, they had more patience and understanding for Sarah's condition. The aide reminded them that Sarah felt frightened and out of control as she became aware of her limitations.

As Sarah's illness progressed, Rachel realized how difficult it would be to care for her mother, especially as she approached the late stages of Alzheimer's. She was ready to relinquish her own need to control the situation, and moved her mother into a local facility specializing in Alzheimer's patients. Jim and Rachel were concerned about the transition for Sarah, but the aide gave them great advice. She suggested having lunch at the facility every day for a week prior to the move. This would help Sarah feel comfortable with the new location. The day of the move, Jim occupied Sarah while Rachel and the movers set up Sarah's room in the facility exactly as it was in their home. That day, as they had been doing all week, Sarah, Rachel, and Jim had lunch at the facility. Instead of going home, they all went to Sarah's new room, set up like her old room, and stayed the day and had dinner together that night. Jim and Rachel met Sarah for breakfast the next morning and Sarah seemed fine. Jim and Rachel joined Sarah for either lunch or dinner every day for the first week she was in the facility, and by week's end, Sarah was content in her new home. Jim and Rachel were relieved that Sarah would now get the attention and help she needed, and they now had time together to talk and renew their bond.

Lessons Learned

Aging is not static. Conditions change and needs change; therefore, we must be willing to adjust our decisions. A decision made last year may have been the right one then, but may need to be revisited the next year. Every case is different, just as every family situation differs.

You will have the best chance of success if you follow these steps:

- Read up on your parent's medical and mental condition.
- Talk to everybody and anybody who has expertise in these areas, and talk to other families in the same boat.
- Visit care facilities.
- Find out exactly what it takes to care for your parent. Consider staying with your parent for a week.
- Soul search to determine if you can effectively care for your parent. If so, can you do it on your own? Do you need outside assistance? In many cases, it is very difficult for a family member to care for an Alzheimer's patient in the late stage of the disease.
- Locate organizations, services, and groups that can help.
- Create a list of available resources. (Use the checklist in the Resource section of this book.)

- Talk to your partner, kids, and family members about what it will mean to move your parent into the home.
- Talk to your parent about moving in. Determine how he would feel. Listen to him. Discuss the logistics: What furniture comes and what goes; what happens to pets and prized collections of possessions. Bring up financial matters: Does he help with bills? Rent?
- Make a family decision. Involve everyone the move will impact.
- Pick a date for the move that gives everyone a chance to adjust.
- Remain open to reassess the living situation and your parent's needs as they change.
- Keep an open heart, and know that you are doing your best.

chapter 5

managing and protecting your parent's assets

How would you feel if, after working for the same company for forty-five years, someone younger with less experience took over, gave away your office, demoted you, took your title, and started telling you what to do? You probably wouldn't give in without a fight. Although moving your parent into your home is not meant to be a hostile takeover, it can come across that way if you aren't careful. When your parent moves in you are, in essence, agreeing to take on many important responsibilities. These responsibilities do not just cover health and physical well-being, but very often trickle into the financial arena as well. Whether you intended to or not, the role of Family Chief Financial Officer (CFO) may be yours.

If you are going to take on the obligation of managing your parent's money, it's best to have an open discussion with everyone involved and come to some agreement about how assets should be handled. In addition, you will best serve all parties if you learn the terms, tools, resources, and financial guidelines necessary to do a good job. If you are in charge, you must be clear on who pays which bills and who ultimately carries out final wishes. This is a tall order, but without discussion and agreement (whether formal or informal) your parent may feel bulldozed by your attempts to take care of her and siblings can feel slighted or even shortchanged in the end. Whenever possible, include other family members in the conversation so you can make your concerns, intentions, and how you would like to help clearly known. Including family members makes your decisions well known and puts everyone on the same team. Prepare, be honest, and don't leave anything to chance.

Unfortunately, Ellie and Ian left everything to chance.

ONE FAMILY'S EXPERIENCE *Ellie and Ian*

My wife, Ellie, and I both have full-time jobs. We have four teenage girls and consider it a special day if we all manage to have dinner together. We're close, but we're always running in different directions. When important matters come up we talk about them on the fly. It was no different the day Ellie brought up moving my mother in with us. Halfway through the discussion we both knew it was a done deal. No big negotiations—no planning. We aren't the Brady Brunch; we don't hold family meetings. We bring up a topic, we decide, we implement. That's about it. For better or for worse, we wing it.

After my mother moved in, I was surprised that she and I had disagreements and even some hard feelings. We had always gotten along well, so I wasn't expecting it. Luckily, we worked through whatever came up. For example, Mom likes a morning cigarette. Our house is strictly nonsmoking. I felt like a heel having my seventy-year-old mother out on the porch in the winter. She was taken aback when I suggested it, and my wife was angry, but that's how I felt. Eventually she got used to going outside, and she forgave me for banishing her to the porch. When it came right down to it, none of that really mattered. All of our disagreements could be worked out and eventually were. However, after about a month, the real problems and issues began to surface, and as it turned out, the real problems were money related.

About a month after the move we started getting bills—for Mom's storage space, for extra cable channels, and for extra phone lines. To top it all off, the gas and electric bills were huge. I hadn't thought about the added expense of an additional housemate—a housemate who is always cold and turning up the heat. We had an increase in the water bill, electricity, phone, gasoline (extra driving from transporting mom to her activities and appointments), groceries, dog food, and so on. I don't mean to complain—we can work through anything—I just wasn't expecting all the money issues we would be facing.

In light of our added expenses, I think she should pay rent and help with the bills. But, it's uncomfortable talking about it now that she already moved in. A couple of weeks ago, Mom had chest pains. We brought her to the emergency room. Thankfully she was fine; however, I realized then that she didn't have a health-care proxy. How could we enforce her wishes if we weren't given legal rights to do so, or for that matter, if we didn't know what they were? I wished we had discussed finances and her estate prior to the move. I didn't realize how many decisions we had to make. Maybe the Brady Bunch was onto something: We should have had a family meeting including my sisters and their husbands and decided all this ahead of time.

Ian and Ellie are like most couples with kids. They are busy and make decisions as issues arise. They don't spend a lot of time pondering what ifs. In many cases, that approach works. However, when it comes to finances the "let's see what happens" approach rarely works out well. Ian and Ellie discovered this a little too late. They found themselves trying to discuss money and end-of-life planning with Beth at a time when she felt extremely vulnerable. She was now living under their roof, and was feeling that she had already lost her autonomy and control over her life. In addition, there was the added pressure of other family members (Ian's sisters) questioning Ian and Ellie's motives because they hadn't been part of the financial decision-making process.

Financial and Legal Eldercare Planning

Senior Resource Center, Inc. (SRC) is a privately held organization that offers care management, financial advising, and overall elder-law guidance for families looking after their elderly parents. Utilizing the services of an eldercare resource center like SRC streamlines the process of gathering financial and legal information as you begin the daunting task of effectively and lovingly caring for your parent and his legal affairs.

Senior care-management organizations will not only work with you to create the best financial plan, but will also help you determine the optimal living environment for your parent by assessing his emotional and physical needs. SRC has used a holistic approach to work with more than 4,000 families over the last several years. They help identify parents' medical needs and the best type of ongoing care and support for the parents as well as family members responsible for caregiving.

Once you have a clear overall picture of what it will take to care for your parent, an eldercare resource center can create a care plan, which may shift and evolve over time as your parent's needs change. A care plan is a structured plan that you will ultimately implement to best care for your parent.

If you are contemplating hiring a care-management service, find out if the fees they charge are one-time fees. This will be to your advantage rather than repaying each time your parent's health condition changes.

An eldercare service walks you through financial planning, legal needs, and organizing strategies for implementing the care plan. They help you wade through and understand myriad available services, resources, programs, and legal options to help you maximize care dollars, safeguard your elderly parent's dignity, and protect your parent's assets.

You may choose to use an eldercare support service, which ends the fragmentation of eldercare options and eliminates the need for you to personally wade through government agencies, Medicare and Medicaid fine print, and legalese of wills and powers of attorney. Or, you may take on that role yourself and follow the steps listed below. Either way, caring for and protecting your parent is best approached in a systematic way. Most families who moved a parent in without organizing finances first regretted it. The biggest shock came to families who were counting on Medicaid for help when their parent became too ill to live with them. In many cases, in order for the parent to be eligible, Medicaid required that they pay their parent back for rent and other expenses their parent paid them while they were living together.

Part I: Preliminary Education and Research
Step 1: Handle any interim or emergency situations
Step 2: Learn eldercare vocabulary

Step 3: Assess parent's short-term and long-term
emotional and physical needs
Step 4: Create an appropriate care plan based on your
parent's needs

Part II: Financial Allocation, Budgeting, and Safeguarding
Step 5: Create a budget and financial statement to
evaluate your parent's resources
Step 6: Use available outside resources and services to
stretch your care dollars
Step 7: Protect your parent by managing assets and
wishes

**Part III: Disseminating Information and Implementing
the Plan**
Step 8: Open a dialogue with family members, including
your parent when possible
Step 9: Implement

Part I: Preliminary Education and Research

Doing research up front will save you time and aggravation in
the long run. In addition, your preparation will allow more
informed communication with doctors and health-care workers, ensuring your parent gets the best care possible.

Handle any Interim or Emergency Situations
Many families consider moving in an aging parent after a
health scare—their parent fell, had a heart attack or stroke,
is at the end of a long battle with a disease, or is experiencing severe memory impairment. Or sometimes, after a doctor

appointment, family members are told that their parent absolutely cannot live alone.

For some families, the crisis is so imminent that they move their parent in with them directly from the hospital or rehab center, without any planning or preparation. If that is true for you, it doesn't mean you are doomed to a life of putting out fires. Once the immediate emergency passes, you can still regroup and make a plan after your parent has moved in that will allow your family to successfully move forward.

Learn Eldercare Vocabulary

Understanding your aging parent's medical and emotional needs is hard enough, but as Family CFO, you are also going to have to familiarize yourself with the entire field of eldercare, including available services, laws, and rights. Speaking with representatives from Medicare, Medicaid, and other eldercare specialist groups can make you feel like you don't speak the language. Effectively gathering information requires that you have a clear conversation with service care providers. Appendix A contains a list of terms you will need to know and will frequently hear as you begin to make your way through the eldercare maze and take on your role as CFO. Once you can speak "eldercare language" with a little more fluency, you will be better equipped to ask the right questions and get the help and support you need.

Assess Parent's Short-Term and Long-Term Emotional and Physical Needs

You may not be a psychologist or a doctor, but if you are the one who has been caring for your parent you probably have a pretty good idea how much help and supervision she needs. Your personal experience, in conjunction with medical experts' opinions and recommendations, are necessary in evaluating your parent's current as well as future requirements. Even if you aren't 100% sure of what it will take to care for your elderly parent, you'll find out shortly after she moves in with you.

Informal eldercare is on the job training. However, as your parent ages, chances are her needs will also change, so you must remain flexible. To determine your parent's short- and long-term physical and emotional needs, you can either hire a professional geriatric care manager (whose services cost approximately $300–$500) to perform a full-scale evaluation or you can take on that role yourself by doing the following:

1. List tasks that you and others already do to care for your parent. Once your parent moves in, it is likely that you may be responsible for the entire list.
2. List any physical caretaking needs your parent has, such as bathing, dressing, and feeding, that she is unable to do on her own.
3. List any personal support needs such as grocery shopping, housekeeping, and laundry.
4. List medications with dosages and times taken. You may also be in charge of monitoring medication on a daily basis.
5. Create a schedule of doctor appointments.
6. Speak to your parent's primary care doctor to find out the nature and prognosis of your parent's condition. You may be fortunate that your parent does not have an illness, but is aging naturally. However, your aging parent may have a progressive disease or ailment that will predictably worsen over time. Find out the details and future prognosis.

7. If applicable, find out the likely path of the disease and make a plan for potential future care. For example, if you know that your parent will be better off in a care facility geared toward those with a similar ailment to your parent's, look into them before the need arises.

8. Determine your parent's emotional state. Your parent's emotional state can either positively or negatively affect her physical health. Careful observation may offer useful information in terms of how your parent is feeling. Is she depressed, lonely, bored, or angry? Is your parent highly social, yet feels isolated? Many families who moved in an elderly parent indicated that they hadn't realized that once the move took place, their parent would look to them for their entire social life and activity. This isn't necessarily good for you or your parent. If your parent truly seems depressed, consult a mental health professional.

9. Look into options to tend to your parent's emotional well-being. For example, there are many senior social centers and activities available. Is one suitable for your parent? If your parent has been social her entire life, it is important to nurture this side to preserve her quality of life and well-being.

10. Commit to ongoing monitoring and adjusting of your assessment to make sure you are on top of changes and new requirements as they arise.

An example of Ellie and Ian's assessment of Beth's short- and long-term prognoses follows:

- Beth is relatively healthy, though she has diabetes and smokes cigarettes. Ian and Ellie must keep in mind that this combination, over time, brings complications. Beth is already has slightly impaired vision as a side effect of her diabetes and can no longer drive.

- Medications need monitoring. Upon speaking with Beth's doctor, Ian and Ellie were told that Beth has poor circulation in her lower legs and feet. She would need to see a doctor monthly to monitor the situation. In addition, Beth was taking a blood thinner, insulin, high blood pressure medicine, and a low dose of an antidepressant. The doctor recommends that she have blood work to check her levels monthly. Unfortunately, the lab and doctor's office are in different locations, so the two visits become a bit of an excursion.

- Beth can perform all of her own daily physical caretaking. She can dress, bathe, use the bathroom, and feed herself; however, she has left the stove on and can be clumsy in the kitchen. Even though Beth protests, Ellie cooks meals ahead of time and leaves sandwiches in the refrigerator so Beth doesn't have to cook. She uses the microwave to heat meals and water for coffee.

- Beth feels isolated in her new home. Beth's doctor is worried that she feels lonely while Ian and Ellie are at work and recommends that at least once a week Beth visit a local senior center where she can play cards and spend the day with others.

You aren't doing your parent any good by denying the truth about her condition. It is common to feel, "Mom is just fine—she takes her medication by herself—she just forgets every now and then." Or, "Mom's hearing is fine— she was never a good listener . . . ." Be truthful and realistic about your parent's abilities and limitation.

The following is a list of questions to ask yourself as you begin to assess your parent's needs. The questions are meant to point out areas you could potentially improve upon to make your home safer for your parent. Use this completed questionnaire as a springboard for communication when you consult with your parent's doctor and other specialists. You can find a copy of the questionnaire in Appendix C.

DAILY LIVING QUESTIONNAIRE			
Task	Yes	Yes with Help	No
Can your parent stand from a seated position?			
Can your parent walk unassisted with a walker or cane?			
Can your parent dress and undress?			
Can your parent bathe and wash?			
Can your parent use the toilet?			
Can your parent prepare meals and eat?			
Can your parent take medication independently, including insulin?			
Can your parent perform diabetes blood testing (if applicable)?			
Can your parent remember to take medication?			
Can your parent tidy her room? Do laundry?			
Can your parent go grocery shopping?			
Can your parent use the telephone or call for assistance?			

questionnaire continued on following page

DAILY LIVING QUESTIONNAIRE

Task	Yes	Yes with Help	No
Can your parent manage her money and pay bills?			
Can your parent manage her schedule (make appointments)?			
Can your parent drive?			

PHYSICAL AND EMOTIONAL WELL-BEING QUESTIONNAIRE

Task	Good	Fair	Poor
How is your parent's memory?			
How is your parent's clarity of thought?			
How is your parent's cognitive ability?			
How is your parent's decision-making process?			
How is your parent's state of mind? Is she depressed?			
How is your parent's vision?			
How is your parent's hearing?			
How is your parent's speech?			
How is your parent's mobility?			
How are your parent's bladder and bowel control?			
How is your parent's heart/blood pressure/cholesterol health?			
How is your parent's joint function? Arthritis?			

ENVIRONMENTAL SAFETY AND COMFORT QUESTIONNAIRE

Task	Okay as Is	Change Required
Well-lit entryways, hallways, and rooms		
Easy-to-reach light switches		
Nonskid strips in the bathtub or shower		
Nonslip bath mats		
Sturdy handrails		
Tacked-down rug edges and corners		
Stairs and hallways clutter free		

FINANCIAL INDEPENDENCE AND PREPAREDNESS QUESTIONNAIRE

Task	Yes	No
Can your parent make deposits?		
Can your parent balance her checkbook?		
Can your parent pay her bills?		
Is your parent aware of her monthly income and expenses?		
Is your parent able to file her taxes?		
Does your parent have a will?		
Has your parent assigned a power of attorney?		
Does your parent have a health-care proxy or living will?		
Was your parent or her spouse a veteran?		
Are your parent's assets organized and definable?		
Is your parent interested in setting up a trust?		

questionnaire continued on following page

FINANCIAL INDEPENDENCE AND PREPAREDNESS QUESTIONNAIRE		
Task	*Yes*	*No*
Has your parent had any estate planning?		
Does your parent have a DNR or other advanced directives?		
Does your parent have long-term care insurance?		

Create an Appropriate Care Plan Based on Your Parent's Needs

A care plan is essential when caring for your elderly parent. The healthier and more independent your parent is, the simpler the plan will be. Many families with a parent who is ill or has many needs may choose to use a care-management service to ensure that all of their parent's needs are addressed in the best possible way. Here is an example of the care plan Ian and Ellie ultimately created for Beth:

1. Doctor appointments (two times per month, with additional appointments throughout the year, such as eye doctor, podiatrist, gastroenterologist, dermatologist, and so on)
2. Haircut and clothes shopping (once a month)
3. Veterinarian appointments for the dogs (twice a year)
4. Oversee Beth's medication (she sometimes forgets to take her pills)
5. Daily monitoring of blood sugar (Beth's impaired vision makes it a little difficult for her to read the monitor)
6. Pay bills, manage finances, and prepare annual taxes

7. Keep up to date on the changing parameters of Medicare and Beth's health insurance
8. Set up a will
9. Arrange get-together times for Beth and her friends and other family members
10. Drop Beth off and pick her up at the local senior center once a week

Overall, this to-do list is fairly simple—for now. Keep in mind that your parent's care plan may not be quite as simple and it is likely to change. However, you will be more in control of the tasks at hand when you are clear on what you need to do and when. In addition, when there is a clear list in hand, it becomes easier to discuss what other family members can do to help.

Part II: Financial Allocation, Budgeting, and Safeguarding

Not all people enjoy financial planning, budgeting, or organizing; however, it is a crucial step in caring for you parent. The plan described below will make the task manageable.

CREATE A BUDGET AND FINANCIAL STATEMENT TO EVALUATE YOUR PARENT'S RESOURCES

The word "budget" sends many people running in the opposite direction. However, a budget is a crucial tool when taking on the role of Family CFO. A budget is simply organizing income and expenses and making sure that the expenses do not exceed income. Use the Budgeting Form in Appendix D to make the process easier.

Even if you have never created a budget or financial statement for you or your family, it is still crucial for your parent to have one. Like it or not, you could ultimately be accountable to the estate, to the government if you are requesting government-funded aid, to your siblings, and to your parent. In addition, a financial statement that contains income, expenses, and assets is required in order to receive any government or charitable services or aid, as well as residency in a nursing home or assisted-living facility. It's best to create the financial statement and budget ahead of time to have on hand. Beyond that, you need the facts and figures to best manage your parent's needs. Once you have a clear picture of your parent's financial strengths and limitations, you may find that she is eligible for state or government assistance or discounts on helpful programs.

As you know, eldercare costs can be astronomical, much of which is not covered by health insurance. Taking advantage of available financial aid and subsidies can be the difference between struggling to care for your parent alone and receiving competent caring assistance from professionals.

The following are examples of typical categories of income. It is likely that your parent has more than one income source. The first step is to find out all avenues of income. Then, list the monthly income from each source. Once you are sure that you have your parent's monthly income figures, move on to the Expense list.

Income Categories
- Social security
- Pension
- Disability
- Alimony

- Annuity
- Interest income and dividends
- Lottery or gambling winnings or prize money
- Retirement disbursements
- Rental income
- Royalties
- Commissions
- Court-mandated reparations
- Veteran's benefits or pensions

The following are examples of typical categories of expenses. Take some time and think about all the possible expenses your parent may have. Don't limit the list to the obvious bills such as utilities; think about all living expenses, which will include clothing, gifts, and entertainment. Once you are sure that you have your parent's total monthly expense figures, move on to the Asset list.

Expense Categories
- Rent/mortgage
- Insurance (car, health, life, long-term care)
- Utilities (phone, electricity, oil, cable)
- Car (payments, fuel, service)
- Clothes
- Food
- Transportation (bus, taxi, train)
- Medical and prescription copays
- Entertainment
- Personal care (haircut, acupuncture, etc.)
- Gifts (holiday, birthday gifts, etc.)
- Household supplies (light bulbs, cleaning detergent, soap, etc.)

- Office expenses (stamps, paper, envelopes, pens, etc.)
- Debt repayment (any loans, unpaid credit cards, mortgages, other obligations)
- Vacation savings
- Pet care
- Memberships, dues, and subscriptions
- Charitable donations
- Lottery tickets

The following are examples of typical assets. An asset is any property that has value. List all of your parent's assets. Once you are sure that you have your parent's total assets, follow the steps to create your parent's financial picture.

Assets
- Home
- Automobile
- Jewelry
- Art
- Cash on hand
- Investments (money market, stocks, bonds, annuity, life insurance policies, etc.)
- Personal property (estimate value)
- Receivables

The process itself is easy. However, when it comes to money matters there are usually emotional components tied to it. Set aside time when you can focus on the task at hand.

You should now have three separate lists of figures: one for income, one for expenses, and one for assets.

Follow these steps:

1. Add the income numbers.
   (Make sure you use monthly numbers for all entries.)
2. Add the expense numbers.
   (Make sure you use monthly numbers for all entries.)
3. Subtract the expenses from the income.
   That number dictates the next course of action.

If your parent's income exceeds her expenses, use the money leftover for additional health-care support, contribution to the household, or whatever makes sense. The decision depends on the strength of your parent's financial position. Is she rich in assets yet income poor? Or is it the other way around?

If your parent's expenses exceed income, then the deficit can be covered through savings or by reducing the amount of expenses. An accountant can be helpful in working with a budget, especially if your parent's income/expense situation is especially complicated. However, with diligence, you can create your parent's budget by yourself.

When gathering asset information, pull together records of all stocks and bonds and bank-statement information and keep all of the account numbers, addresses, and phone numbers together in a safe place. This process is the same for liabilities. Make sure you have loan and mortgage account numbers and contact information together as well as credit card account numbers and monthly bill information organized and in the same safe place. You will want easy access for managing of your parent's finances. The following page shows Beth's Financial Statement and Budget since she moved in with Ian and Ellie. Appendix D has a blank copy of the form.

FINANCIAL STATEMENT

Income Source	Monthly Dollar Amount
Social Security	$1,425.00
Pension	$713.00
Interest Income	$900.00
Total Income	**$3,038.00**
Expense Source	Monthly Dollar Amount
Mortgage	
Telephone	$32.00
Personal products	$25.00
Health insurance	$456.25
Clothing	$100.00
Transportation	$50.00
Gifts	$75.00
Restaurants and entertainment	$125.00
Knitting supplies	$40.00
Vacation	$175.00
Taxes	$350.00
Medical and prescription copays	$375.00
Professional services	$62.50
Dry cleaning	$12.00
Subscriptions and memberships	$6.50
Vet	$25.00
Pet food and supplies	$30.00
Senior center	$12.50
Misc.	$100.00
Total Expenses	**$2051.75**
Total Cash Flow ($3038.00 - $2051.75)	**$986.25**
Assets	Dollar Amount
Sale of house	$150,000
Retirement in Money Market	$25,000
Stocks and bonds	$10,000
Cash on hand	$1,000
Personal property	$10,000
Total Assets	**$196,000**

As you can see, Beth is in a strong financial position now that she is living with Ian and Ellie; it was more difficult for her to make ends meet when she was living on her own. With the mortgage, taxes, utilities, food, home management, and upkeep she was spending more than she was earning and had to dig into her savings every month, which wasn't good. Even if she hadn't moved in with Ian and Ellie, she would eventually been forced to sell her house. Now that she has sold her home and lives with her children, she has a positive cash flow and can afford to contribute to her new household. Having been used to falling short every month, she was initially defensive and uncomfortable discussing money. But having the actual figures at hand assuaged her fears, and she was more than happy to contribute to the new household. She can preserve her nest egg in case she ultimately needs additional care or supervision.

Use Available Outside Resources and Services to Stretch Your Care Dollars

Because you have decided to have your parent live with you, this section focuses solely on caring for your parent while she is living in your home. No focus will be placed on assisted-living or nursing-home care costs. At this point in your care assessment process, you probably know what your parent needs to maintain independence, health, and a happy life. You have also, at least informally, looked over your parent's finances. If your parent is physically and mentally strong, she may not need more assistance than living with your family offers. However, if she does need additional financial help, you will know how much your parent can afford after putting together a budget.

The following is a list of potential services that are less expensive than private home health care and that can aid in the quality of your parent's life.

Non-nursing private home health care can cost anywhere from $12.00–$25.00 per hour and is rarely covered by insurance. Nursing care can be covered as long as it is doctor prescribed and falls under one of the categories of coverable services.

Outside Resources

Senior centers. Town- or city-sponsored centers are usually free. Privately run centers cost $50–$300 annually. Senior centers are not covered by insurance.

Adult day centers. Cost $30–$75 per day and are not usually covered by Medicare, though many families say it is worth the out-of-pocket cost.

Volunteer services. Free or subsidized, depending on your parent's financial statement.

Religious organization support. Free or subsidized, depending on your parent's financial statement.

Nonprofit organizations. Free or subsidized, depending on your parent's financial statement.
- **Respite care.** The cost of respite care depends on the agency that supplies it. At times it can be covered by insurance.
- **Informal caregiving such as family members and friends.** Free, unless a family member uses eldercare as his profession.

In addition to outside resources, there are other ways to cut eldercare costs without cutting quality of care and services. As most elderly Americans are aware, the cost of prescription drugs can be crippling, with or without health insurance coverage. There are many state-run drug assistance programs (*www.helpingpatients.org*). Call local offices for the aging to discuss other options and see Appendix B for resource numbers and website addresses. The following list is just the beginning of ways to cut prescription drug costs:

- Research state-funded drug assistance programs: Visit NCLS.org to find a list of pharmaceutical assistance programs.
- Use generic brands of pharmaceuticals: *www.pillbot.com.*
- Apply for direct-cost reduction from pharmaceutical companies: *www.rxassist.org* has a comprehensive list of drug companies offering free or discount prescriptions to low-income people, and *www.medicareadvocacy.org* has questions and answers regarding discount drug cards and programs.

In addition to cutting pharmaceutical costs, there are many discounts available to seniors. Consider joining the American Association of Retired Persons (AARP) for a comprehensive list of available discounts to movies, restaurants, shopping, AAA, transportation, vacations, retail stores, and so on. There are also some services covered by insurance. Check with your insurance company to see what services they cover. Be creative and open minded in your search for assistance with caring for your parent. There are more options than you may think!

Protect Your Parent by Managing Assets and Wishes

The typical American holds several misconceptions:

- There will be plenty of time later to plan for illnesses and disabilities.
- Health insurance or Medicaid will pay for nursing-home or long-term care.
- My children will be able to take care of me so I don't need long-term care insurance or have to worry about a nursing home.
- I don't want to deal with estate planning; it is too difficult to think about. Plus, my kids get along; they'll take care of it when the time comes.

It would take an encyclopedia-sized book (and potentially a law degree) to thoroughly discuss and dispel these myths. Thinking and planning ahead is a must. You may ultimately decide to contact experts in elder law and estate planning or you may decide to use your accountant or lawyer. Or, you may decide to sift through it yourself. That is completely up to you. However, to be an effective Family CFO, you will have to familiarize yourself with the following:

- The financial truth about nursing homes and nursing care
- Being in charge
- Medicare and Medicaid basics
- Long-term care insurance options
- Worst-case scenarios
- End-of-life and legacy planning

Nursing Homes and Nursing Care

There are approximately 2 million Americans over the age of sixty-five living in nursing homes. That number is expected to increase by at least 1 million over the next twenty years. The average cost of long-term care facilities averages $40,000–$80,000 per year (expected to rise to $180,000 by 2030) and only about 40 percent of Americans are covered under Medicare and other low-income funding sources. This leaves 60 percent of the people to pay for their long-term care out of pocket. Since 70 percent of Americans are said to have no major long-term financial plan other than a simple will, hundreds of thousands of senior citizens and their families who do not have a large nest egg, long-term care insurance, rich benefactors, or generous monthly incomes can find themselves in a financial crisis.

The federal government's General Accounting Office (GAO) estimates that 43 percent of all Americans will eventually need some form of nursing care during their lifetime, which makes paying for the cost of caring for our aging parents a nationwide concern. Nursing care is not exclusive to residency at a nursing home; it covers skilled nursing at your home after surgery or during recovery from an illness. What would happen if your parent needed six months of nursing care in your home and it is not covered by long-term care insurance? The cost could easily reach $30,000 out of pocket.

Creating a solid financial plan for your parent (as well as for yourself) can potentially safeguard your parent's assets as well as your own future.

Take Charge

If you are taking on the role of Family CFO, you can't do it on the fly or wait until later. Decide to do it and do it right.

(You'll also want to discuss the decision with other members of the family to ensure that you have everyone's support.) That decision, however, is only step 1. Step 2 is gathering the legal paperwork so you can actually take on the job. The following are the five most important legal documents to effectively perform your tasks as CFO:

1. Durable power of attorney, which gives you the legal right to make financial decisions and sign checks and documents on your parent's behalf
2. Health-care proxy (see page 204 for definitions)
3. Living will (see page 205 for definitions)
4. Wills (see page 211 for definitions)
5. Trusts (see page 211 for definitions)

Once your documents are in order, gather all financial information including bank accounts, insurance policies, debts, receivables, and assets. You are probably going to make deposits, write and sign checks, make financial decisions, file tax returns, and consolidate credit card debt. Be diligent; schedule time every month to make sure these tasks don't slip through the cracks.

Long-Term Care Insurance Options

Long-term care insurance picks up where health insurance, Medicare, and Medicaid fall short. Long-term care insurance covers nursing home and other care services for people unable to care for themselves. It includes care for your elderly parent while he is living at home or in your house. It is never too early or too late to consider long-term care insurance. Long-term care can cost anywhere from $100 to $200 or more per day on a short-term or outpatient basis or up to $80,000 a year

Bibliothèque et Archives nationales du Québec

Nom de l'abonné : Dahir Ilhan Ismail
Numéro d'abonné : 02002004536482

Titre : When your parent moves in : every adult
No de document : 32002512711043
Date de retour : 2010-04-04 @ 23:59:00
Cote :
Famille

Titre : Au temps des catastrophes : résister à l
No de document : 32002511858183
Date de retour : 2010-04-04 @ 23:59:00
Cote :
Sciences humaines et sociales

Nombre total de documents : 2

2010-03-14 13:53

Cote :

Nombre de document(s) : 2

Nous vous remercions d'avoir utilisé le guichet
de prêt en libre-service (Guichet # 3).

for nursing home or permanent long-term care. The insurance itself can cost anywhere from $100–$12,000 per year depending on age and benefit options. Therefore, unless the person has saved a great deal of money, long-term care insurance may be a good option.

Long-term care insurance can have many benefits, but it is not for everyone. Contact your insurance agent to discuss the different types of policies, costs, and benefits. If you would like to consider your parent's likelihood to actually need long-term care by the findings from the National Centers for Health Care Statistics, take the National Nursing Home Survey. Either contact The Long Term Care Statistics Branch (301) 458-4747 or visit *www.cdc.gov.*

Medicare and Medicaid Basics

Medicare and Medicaid are complicated, and are not the same. Medicare is available for any person who is sixty-five or older and is eligible to receive social security benefits. Medicaid is a federal/state welfare program that is designed to pay for a range of care such as medical, nursing home, and home health aides for those who are unable to pay for it themselves. There are strict requirements for eligibility such as age, income, assets, health, and family status. Medicare does not provide long-term care, but rather provides short-term medical benefits. Medicaid does cover long-term care, but is a federal welfare program for the poor and needy.

There are very strict guidelines to be eligible for Medicaid. For example, an elderly person requiring full-time care may not qualify for Medicaid even though he may not have enough money to cover food, shelter, prescriptions, and home health care. Medicaid may look at his income as sufficient and deem him ineligible, though he can't pay his bills. Many senior citizens are faced with the decision to completely spend down assets, set up trusts, asset disbursement, and protection, and gifting to become poor enough on paper to qualify for Medicaid. Visit *www.medicaid.com* for more information. As Family CFO, it will be your responsibility to become educated about Medicare and Medicaid.

Worst-Case Scenarios

No one likes to think about what could possibly go wrong. However, as Family CFO you don't have the luxury of hoping for the best without planning for the worst. It would be devastating if your parent had a heart attack, accident, or stroke. It would be even worse if one of those medical catastrophes occurred and you weren't able to care for your parent and ensure that his wishes were carried out. A few legal documents could empower you to honor your parent's desires and help you maintain his rights and dignity. Although your parent (or you, for that matter) may not want to face difficult possibilities, it is your job to take care of your parent, difficult or not.

Consider speaking to your parent about creating a living will. A living will is a document that lets family and medical caregivers know what types of lifesaving measures your parent has approved. And it allows your parent to decide who will be in charge of ensuring his wishes are carried out. A lawyer or eldercare specialist can draft a living will, or you can research online and look into legal websites and draft your own (*www.legalzoom.com, www.lawmart.com, www.living trustsontheweb.com.*) The living will can include health-care proxies, advanced directives, DNR, etc. (See Appendix A for definitions.)

End-of-Life and Legacy Planning

Like it or not, at some point, we all face our mortality. Our legacy to the world is the impact we have made on those we have come in contact with, what we have taught and shared with others, and what we leave to our loved ones to remember us by. As Family CFO, it is beyond the scope of your job to affect the impact your parent has made during his lifetime. However, you can help carry out your parent's legacy by ensuring that his assets and sentimental treasures are given to those he has selected. The last thing you want to do is allow probate or the government to make those decisions. You also want to avoid sibling squabbling at a time when reminiscing and honoring your parent is more appropriate.

You can use your lawyer or eldercare specialists or you can research online to create wills, durable powers of attorney, trusts, guardianships, and so on. Listen to your parent: Who does he want to handle his estate? Who does he want to give his fishing gear to? How about his late wife's favorite ring that he saved? Ask. It will be up to you to make the process as easy as possible. Once the documents are created everyone can rest easy.

Part III: Disseminating Information and Implementing the Plan

It is never easy to discuss end-of-life issues; however, avoiding the discussions will not make the need disappear. Opening the lines of communication will help you best care for your parent with the support of your family.

Open a Dialogue with Family Members

Include your parent in the dialogue whenever possible. Most effective relationships begin with clear communication, and a relationship with your parent or siblings is no different. Have an honest conversation; don't wait until it is too late. Bring up your concerns and talk about issues before they escalate. Having a budget in hand is a great springboard for discussion. It takes the financial matters out of the emotional realm and puts them where they belong—in the practical arena.

An open discussion requires that you talk honestly about your expectations. This is also important when two adult households merge. An open discussion will allow you to see whether or not you have compatible lifestyles, goals, personal habits, spending tendencies, and so on. Your relationship with your parent can impact your life the same as any other important relationship. Make sure you start out on the right foot to prevent any potential misunderstandings.

Implement

You have gathered all the information you need and have put together a viable plan to best care for your aging parent, but taking action and implementing the plan can bring up fear, sadness, anxiety, stress, and just plain old resistance. In some cases, caring for an elderly parent feels like a full-time job. Implementing the plan can mean a major life change for the adult child doing the caretaking. Many families caring for their elderly parent also found it difficult to implement a major change because it signified an end they weren't ready to face.

Think of eldercare preparation like filing taxes. You may not want to think about it; however, eventually you have no choice but to prepare, file, and pay. Implementing your parent's care plan is the same. In the long run, when everyone knows their roles, responsibilities, and potentially what's to come, it will give security and comfort to you, your family, and your parent.

Lessons Learned

Whether self-appointed or elected by default, the job as Family CFO can be tough—especially because it can feel like a full-time job in itself, which you will be managing along with your career and full-time parenting. Your best bet is to get organized and be prepared. You can't plan for everything, but you can do your best with whatever comes your way. Remember:

- Put your cards on the table. Your parent and other family members will feel more comfortable if they know you are being aboveboard, that you have no secret agenda; you just want to care for your parent. Coming up with a contract to cover roles, responsibilities, and expectations is a great way to begin your job.
- Treat each other respectfully during your discussions. Caring for an elderly parent can be difficult and emotional. Remember that no matter how difficult the conversations become, you all love each other and want what's best.
- Avoid unilateral decisions. Whenever possible, try to get a family consensus. It will avert hard feelings and distrust down the road.

- Put together a financial statement and budget. It is always easier to make decisions when everyone is working with the same facts; numbers don't lie. You will have an easier time coming to a consensus when you are starting from the same place. Once you have numbers in front of you, it will be easier to discuss how you would like your parent to contribute to your household. It will also give you a realistic idea of what she can and can't afford.
- You don't have to plan every single detail, and don't expect everything to work out perfectly. Keep educating yourself and be flexible when circumstances change.
- Just because you are CFO doesn't make you the boss. Remember that your parent and siblings are all adults and want to be treated that way.
- Discuss the hard stuff up front. Set up estate planning such as POAs, trusts, wills, health-care proxies, living wills, and end-of-life wishes. Make sure you are clear on what your parent wants and how she would like the estate handled. It may be uncomfortable, but it is important to talk about.
- Weigh your options. Look into the many resources available to your parent including long-term care insurance, Medicare, Medicaid, subsidized assistance, and so on. Decide what best suits your parent's individual needs.

Always remember you are not alone. Caring for an aging parent can be one of life's most challenging circumstances, but there are resources available to help. Be prepared, learn the language, do your homework, love your parent, and ultimately, trust that you will do your best.

chapter 6

the big move

THE BIG MOVE IS JUST THAT—BIG. It's emotionally and logistically big. Prepare yourself. There will be shuffling of long-standing roles—who is head of the household now? There are two households of stuff fitting into one house. In some cases, there will be two households of pets. Do you bring your dad's favorite antique sofa into your contemporary house? How will you park a third car in the two-car driveway? In addition to the luggage, boxes, china, and books, don't forget to pack the emotional baggage of your parent-child relationship (because, like it or not, that comes on the truck as well).

Nancy and the Reynolds family found out the hard way just how emotionally difficult the process of moving can be.

ONE FAMILY'S EXPERIENCE *Nancy and Molly*

My husband's mom, Molly, was getting older. She was in good health, but Rick was concerned about her and wanted me to consider moving her in with us. I thought it was a good idea, especially since Molly was feeling lonely after her husband's

death. I really didn't think she'd go for it because she lived in
her house for forty-five years. Surprisingly, Molly agreed to the
move. The deciding factor was that her best friend and next-
door neighbor announced she was moving to Arizona to be
closer to her children. There really was nothing keeping Molly in
her home anymore, and she wanted to be part of a family again.
She was ready and excited about this next chapter in her life.

Once we were all on the same page, it was time to start
packing Molly's house for the move. I approached it just like
I approach everything: I got down to business. My kids wanted
to help, so I assigned each a room to pack and gave instructions to make sure every box was clearly labeled: Red label—
bring to our house; green label—storage; black label—give
away; blue label—throw away. My kids tried to tell me Grandma
was getting upset during the packing, but moving is a lot of
work. In addition, Molly collected so many things over the
years—dishes, dolls, doilies, magazines, crystal swans—that
I wanted to weed through and streamline the process. I couldn't
have all that stuff in my house, could I? So, I spent two weeks
sorting, boxing, labeling, throwing away, and giving away.

I thought I was doing the right thing by efficiently handling
my mother-in-law's move. According to my husband and kids,
I made every possible mistake.

Looking back, I can see I made some pretty big ones.
I shouldn't have banished Molly from the process. I was just
trying to make it easier for her, but that was wrong. I ended
up making unilateral decisions about which of her things were
important and which weren't. I should have asked her because
I got it wrong a lot of the time. I think I might even have put a
damper on her excitement to live with us.

It all came to a head the morning after the move when she
wanted a cup of coffee. For the past twenty years, Molly had

her coffee in a cup she and Dad bought while vacationing in St. Martin. This was her routine and it gave her comfort. I thought it was a silly looking cup and I put it in storage. Molly didn't want to upset anyone, but I could see her fuming on the inside.

Luckily, as time passed and we began settling into the new living arrangement, Molly created new routines and ultimately forgave me. But I know I could have made this transition go more smoothly if I had remembered how difficult this change was for Molly and had respected her attachment to her things.

It bears repeating: This move is big. It may seem like a natural decision if your family is the kind that stuffs thirty people in the house for Thanksgiving and always welcomes "strays." However, the very nature of the move for your parent requires that you treat it with care. A few callous or thoughtless decisions about your parent's possessions can cause emotional distress and hard feelings. Just because everyone agrees to the move doesn't make it easier. It may seem like a burden—arranging the details of the move, getting the house Grandma ready, and orchestrating movers, storage, and change of address forms—but to your parent it is more than a big to-do list. It is the beginning of a new life, but also the loss of an old one. Your mother's possessions may be her link to her life and past as she knew it. Change, even for the better, is challenging for most people, especially change that alters the course of your life.

Making the Move Less Stressful for Your Parent

Don't be in such a hurry to check items off your to-do list. Even if it takes a little longer, let your parent be part of the decision-making process. Gently remind your parent that all of his belongings may not fit into your house. Find out which items are most important; let him tell you which of his items have sentimental value. Let him tell you which items he wants to bring, what he would like to store or give away and to whom, and which items he might be ready to sell or donate. Including your parent in all aspects of moving may double the time it takes to complete the move, but that goodwill gesture will go a long way toward a smooth transition.

Luckily for Nancy, Molly knew that underneath all the business of the move, Nancy and Rick were motivated to create a new expanded family and for all of them to live together in love and harmony. And in the end, they did.

As in Nancy and Molly's case, problems can arise during a move if you and your parent are at odds or fighting over things. However, even bigger problems can arise when siblings fight over the parent's possessions during the move. This is what happened with Bill and his children.

ONE FAMILY'S EXPERIENCE *Liz and Bill*

Where were my brothers when Dad was in the hospital after his stroke? My husband, Ken, and I were with him every day. Now that Dad has been released from the rehab facility, we don't think he should live on his own. We want to keep an eye on him, so we are moving him in with us. Dad agreed the second we brought up the idea—he didn't like being alone. Once again, Bill Jr. and Eddie are too busy to help. That's okay; Ken and I can take care of Dad. We want to take care of him.

So, Ken, Dad, and I started the move by going room to room in the house deciding what to do with his furniture, books, music, pictures, clothes, and so on. He didn't have a lot, but what he did have was nice, even though he wasn't particularly attached to most of it. He had some of Mom's personal things that he wanted to keep because he said that they reminded him of her. We made sure to bring them with us. Other than that, Dad trusted me with the details. I loved hearing him say, "Liz, you're a good daughter." He knew he was in good hands; I would never let him down.

We wanted Dad to feel comfortable in our house, so we were planning to set up his bedroom exactly as it was in his own house. We hoped that it would ease the transition for him. We all knew the move was the right decision, but I will tell you, my heart just about broke when the movers took out the last boxes, leaving the home I grew up in empty. Mom was gone and my childhood home was for sale. It would have been nice if my brothers had shown up to offer a little help or support.

The moving day went as expected, but I had no idea that this was the beginning of some less than friendly exchanges that would occur between me and my brothers. When we arrived at the storage facility, Bill Jr. and Eddie were there. Ironically, with antiques on the line, they weren't too busy anymore.

I had always been the one to care for my father. My brothers never helped. Of course I expected to be the one to handle the details of who gets what when the time came. I wasn't going to keep everything, but I was not happy that my brothers swooped down like vultures on the day of the move.

When I got to the storage space my brothers, Bill Jr. and Eddie, were there. Eddie immediately began to take over. He started talking to the movers, asking if they could make a pit stop at his house, which was just down the road. He was questioning me and my decisions, and making leading statements to Dad: "Hey Dad, you don't want to pay hundreds a month for storage do you? Not only that, who knows what can happen to your antiques here? Why don't I just take them to my house and look after them? Okay?" Dad didn't know what to say or what to do. He was just happy to see his sons because they barely visited. This put me in a terrible situation.

The Importance of Possessions

Moving day is emotional for everyone concerned. It isn't the time to corner your parent or start haggling over her possessions. This is not to say you shouldn't decide with your parent who gets what ahead of time, but moving day isn't the time to do so.

It's common for an elderly parent to begin giving away valuables and money during her lifetime—that can make it easier upon her death. This is especially true if siblings, children, or relatives don't get along and are all vying for an inheritance. Unfortunately, sibling disagreements over a parent's money and possessions are very, very common. Therefore, coming up with a game plan in advance can offset many potential problems down the road and help you maintain a healthy relationship with your siblings and other family members, even when the inevitable arguments arise. It might seem harsh to "rehearse" your parent's death by deciding on her possessions while she is alive; however, as morbid as it may seem, it can actually aid in creating family harmony.

When caring for an aging parent, a conversation about who gets what is uncomfortable but inevitable. Once there is a will or a binding written agreement, then you can go back to having the kind of relationship where division of property and the anxiety that goes along with it isn't an issue. Unfortunately, sometimes the will itself or the parent's wishes create family rifts. Only you can decide what course of action or emotional stance is right for you to take when dealing with family member's dissatisfaction with their lot; hopefully, in time everyone will learn to accept the wishes of your parent.

Moving Logistics

A relatively successful move begins weeks, if not months, before the movers show up. Depending on your parent's condition, you may not have the luxury of months to orchestrate the details of the move, but you can make the most of the time you do have.

Make a Plan
Planning the move ahead of time, no matter how much time you have, can streamline the move itself. Pick a date, the mover, and determine responsibilities such as who packs, who is present at your parent's house, who is in charge of storage, and who helps Grandpa set up his room. There are a lot of details to consider.

If possible, ask your parent where he wants to be the day of the move. He might want to be part of the process or he may find it too difficult, depending on his condition and circumstances that precipitated the move. Maybe a family member will take him to lunch or to a movie. Whatever you decide, make sure he is not alone.

Decide when your parent will move into your house. Just because the move hasn't happened, doesn't mean your parent can't come and stay with you. If your parent is coming before the move itself, he might feel more comfortable using his own sheets and towels and some personal items so he doesn't feel like a guest in your home.

Decide where things go. It might be too stressful for your parent to pack up his things, but in many cases he will be happy to let you know what he'd like to have with him in his new home. Bring colored stickers and go room to room with him and let him talk about his possessions, where he got them, and what they mean to him. Assign color codes for each destination (storage, his new home, donation, and so on). As you walk and talk, place the appropriate color stickers on items or closet doors. This will not only make packing much easier, but will allow your parent to share stories and reminisce with you. In addition, your parent will not have to decide, under duress, if he'd like to keep an item. If he is uncertain about a particular item, he can always think about it and place the sticker a little later.

Pack. Once all items are designated, it is time to pack. Packing can take days or weeks depending on how much your parent has. Make sure you bring enough boxes, magic markers, tape, newspaper to wrap delicate items, trash bags, and labels. The moving company will most likely sell you boxes or you can go to a local liquor or grocery store to pick up some for free. Write the contents on the outside of each box along with where the box will ultimately go (storage, bedroom, living room, etc.). If possible, group all boxes going to the same location together. This will speed up the moving process and probably save time when the movers are unloading the truck. Since the move will most likely take place a few days after you have packed, if your parent plans to stay in his home until that day, make sure you leave out a few pots, place settings, sheets and towels, and a suitcase full of clothes for him to wear.

Arrange for the house or apartment to be cleaned. After the move, consider having a plan to have the house or apartment cleaned. You and your family can do it or have a service come.

Discuss finances, legal documents, and bequeathments. Whenever possible, the best time to secure financial arrangements and legal documents is prior to the move. This way, your parent still feels a sense of independence when making difficult decisions. This also alleviates the problems that Liz and Bill had on the day of the move. In addition, once your parent moves in with you, you are responsible for his health and well-being. You will want to make sure you have legal right to care for him according to his wishes.

Cancel utilities, file change of address forms, and send out notices to friends and family. You can call utility companies ahead of time with a cancellation date. You can also have the post office forward your parent's mail. Your parent has most likely been in his home for many years and it would make sense to send out a letter to his friends and relatives letting them know where they can reach him.

Set up a new phone. If your parent will have his own phone number, have it set up and working prior to the move. This way, the evening that he is in his new bedroom, he can pick up the phone and make a call. Or you can arrange for friends to call him. Receiving phone calls is one way for a person to feel at home.

Fill the refrigerator and pantry with foods your parent likes. Food can be comforting. Your parent will feel cared about if he wants a snack and the crackers that he always eats are there.

Acknowledge the significance of the day and have a celebratory meal when the day is done. Have a family celebration welcoming your parent into your home. Make sure all the kids can make it. Any gesture to ensure your parent knows he is wanted and welcomed will go a long way.

Lessons Learned

Preparation for the move is just as important, if not more so, than the moving day itself. It is all stressful; there is no getting around it. However, the better prepared you are, the easier it will be on everyone. You'll have to deal with logistics, movers, furniture placement, new pets in the house, and broken or lost artifacts.

Elderly parents making the move will also have a lot to deal with. However, their struggle will include saying goodbye to a home they've likely known for years. They will no longer be head of the house. They will no longer have final say, and their rules will now take a back seat to yours. Sure, they will build a new life, but it doesn't alleviate the mourning and adjustment period. Preparation makes the day easier for you; however, to make the move truly successful for your parent, you must include her in the decision making whenever possible. Let her decide how her room will be set up, what items she would like to have, what clothes to bring, what to store, what to give away. Make sure your refrigerator is filled with foods that she likes to eat on the day of the move. This way, the moment she is moved in, Grandma can have her favorite coffee and bagels. A joint effort and thoughtfulness will preserve a great deal of independence and dignity for your parent.

An added stress to the day is that previously disinterested relatives can come out of the woodwork, and in many cases their agenda is to protect their own interests. The most successfully transitioning families' parents had already created a clear will laying out the inheritance details ahead of time.

Ultimately, no matter how difficult the transition, how many uncomfortable conversations and confrontations you have, how many items are broken or lost, or even how cluttered your house looks when your parent's things have been brought into your home, remember that your desire to care for your parent will bring you through the difficult times and to a place where you are living together as peacefully as possible.

chapter 7

your newly expanded family

YOU'VE MADE THE decision—your parent is moving in. What will it be like? Will it be like that time your Dad came to visit for three weeks? Oh no, not that! By the end of his stay you were ready to kill each other. Or will it be like the time you all went to Disney together? That was great! Everyone had a wonderful time, especially when Dad volunteered to watch the kids, giving you and your spouse the chance to have a long-overdue date. Which is it? The answer is, neither. When Dad moves in, it is an entirely new scenario, unlike anything you have experienced before, and so you must treat it differently.

Having a parent move in with you will change your life, not necessarily for the better or for the worse. It will, however, permanently change the dynamic of your family. You must be prepared. Preparation and properly managed expectations will allow you to take control of how the change affects you and your family, positively and negatively. Denial will bring disappointment and hard feelings. Look what happened to Jennifer and Tom.

ONE FAMILY'S EXPERIENCE *Jennifer and Tom*

Jennifer and her husband, Tom, spent the last year weighing the idea of moving Tom's seventy-five-year-old mother, Mary, into their home. Tom and Jennifer are both detail oriented and weren't about to rush into any decision without a clear plan in place. Once they had worked through all the details of Mary's move, they set their plan in motion. They called a Realtor to put her house up for sale and met with a contractor to begin designing and building a small addition on their home in which Mary would live.

To everyone's surprise, the first weekend's open house brought an offer for the full asking price. The buyers would be ready to close and move in within two months. However, the contractor ran into scheduling delays and had to push the start of Mary's addition out for six weeks, leaving a three- to four-month period before she could move into the addition. So Jennifer offered their guestroom until the addition was ready.

They made the necessary adjustments and the move itself all took place without a hitch. However, the adjustment to the new living arrangement hit a few snags. Because Mary was living in the guest room, she couldn't relax. She felt like she was living out of a suitcase. She also didn't want to intrude, make too much noise, or interrupt Tom and Jennifer's schedule. There were a few problems, but they weren't getting too worked up about it since they all assumed that once the addition was finished they would settle into the new arrangement. This assumption, however, would turn out to be a bigger problem than they had anticipated. Tom, Jennifer, and Mary all saw their current circumstance as temporary, so they never worked toward making the new living arrangement gel. Instead, they were all on company behavior.

A few months later, construction dragged on and the addition still wasn't complete. Jennifer could see that Mary was somewhat stressed and assured her that everything was fine: "Mary, please, relax and make yourself at home!" Jennifer meant it in the moment, but was surprised how "make yourself at home" would play out. One day, Jennifer noticed Mary's figurines displayed in the living room, the kitchen cupboards rearranged, and a couple of new afghans were tossed over the back of the sofa. Jennifer decided not to say anything—Mary would be moving into the addition anytime now. The figurines and the other small changes Mary made really weren't a problem. The real problem for Jennifer was that Mary greeted her each day when she arrived from work wanting to help make dinner, which created an enforced sit-down dinner schedule. Jennifer was always on a diet. She didn't necessarily want to have a sit-down dinner. Tom's work schedule was unpredictable and he didn't like the pressure of having to be home by 7:00. However, they accommodated Mary. She was, after all, a guest in their home.

One year later, with tensions running still higher, the addition was finally complete. Relieved, they went out to dinner and celebrated. Mary was excited to have her own space and to finally unpack. Tom and Jennifer were looking forward to some privacy and their old schedule. They spent the weekend moving and arranging furniture in the addition, until Mary thought it looked just right. The space was beautiful.

The next night Jennifer rushed home from work, looking forward to a salad in front of the television. When she stepped through the door she felt like she walked right into a wall. Mary was sitting on the sofa, just as she had for the last year. Sweetly looking up at Jennifer she said, "Ready to make dinner?" Speechless and confused, Jennifer poured herself a glass of wine—a really big glass.

Jennifer and Tom wanted Mary to move in with them. However, Jennifer was emotionally unprepared for the actuality of the new living arrangement. When Mary first moved into their guest room, Jennifer saw the living arrangement as temporary, which it was. Therefore, while Mary was in the guest room, Jennifer was not focused on creating a new family unit, but on Mary moving out. But Mary was never going to move out; she was just going to move out of the guest room and into another part of the house. When the addition was finally finished and Mary moved into it, Jennifer hadn't shifted her thinking from, "Mary is a guest in our home" to "Mary lives with us, and she is part of our family."

Your Parent Is a Member of the Family— Not a Guest

During the interviews we conducted, families able to smoothly transition a parent into their home all spoke of the new housemate using similar language. They referred to their parent as part of the family. They used affectionate terminology reflective of an extended family unit. Not one of the families describing a relatively positive transition referred to their parent as a guest or visitor. Their language choice and dialogue about their parent revealed their underlying attitude and level of acceptance for the new living arrangement. Jennifer, on the other hand, referred to Mary as a guest, and wrongly assumed that the addition on the house would create two separate living environments, with the understanding that Mary would live exclusively in her part and would be a guest in the main house. She assumed that her mother-in-law would have a separate life, scheduling visits as if she lived down the road.

Jennifer was wrong. The moment Mary sold her home and moved into theirs, she didn't see herself as a guest, but as an extended member of the household, even more so after Jennifer explicitly told Mary to make herself at home.

A guest is a visitor to whom you extend hospitality. "Visitor" is the key word. A guest stays with you for the short term; they may hang a few things in the closet, leave their toothbrush in the bathroom, but they do not live with you, they visit you. Inviting someone to live with you is long-term. When you invite a parent to live with you, assume that you are gaining a new housemate. He will show up for dinner, join you in the living room, may want to put things around the house, and is not leaving any time soon. Scrupulously avoiding the word "guest" is not going to get you off the hook. Don't get caught up in semantics. You know whether or not you feel your parent is part of the family, or if you see him as an intrusion when he regularly joins the family for dinner. When your parent moves in—he's in.

The fact that your parent may live in an addition doesn't change that—the addition is still part of your home. Families who did not build an addition had an easier time with the transition because it was clear right up front that Dad wasn't going to be sequestered in his room until invited to come out. The new living arrangement was evident. The difficulties were in setting boundaries and making new rules, just like all families when they move in a parent.

Most (but certainly not all) families interviewed that built an addition on their home for the purposes of having their parent close, but still separate, were caught off guard. They were surprised to find that while their parent may have stored their possessions in the addition and slept in the addition, he wanted to spend most of his time in the main house with the rest of the family. The transition into the addition, as opposed to a room in the house, actually proved more difficult for some families because they held onto the idea of guest versus housemate for a longer time. They seemed to have different expectations than those who moved a parent into a spare room. Looking in from the outside, it is a natural assumption that the parent would want to be with the family. That is, after all, why he gave up his home and moved in.

Properly preparing for the new living arrangement requires creating new household rules. In addition, don't overlook the mental and physical adjustments required for this new living situation. The following are some of the necessary mental shifts needed to successfully create your new family unit.

Mental Adjustments

Above all, it's important to accept your parent as a member of the family. If you use the word "guest," you will ultimately feel that your parent is intruding. You will be less likely to work on creating a new family dynamic, while holding onto the old one. This doesn't mean that your parent owns the house or has equal say in rule making, home decorating, maintenance, whether or not pets are allowed, or if she can smoke in the living room. It is your home; however, it is your parent's home too and she belongs, just like your children belong. She doesn't have final say, but she does have a right to be there.

There were many ways that Jennifer and Tom could have helped Mary feel more like a member of the family. One way was to simply tell her the truth. For example, Mary likes to have a sit-down dinner; Tom and Jennifer don't, so accommodating Mary every night created unspoken tension. They could have treated her like a member of the family and just said, "Sit-down dinners are great, but Jennifer is on a diet half the time and I don't know what time I'm going to get home from work. Why don't we just fend for ourselves, and once a week or so we'll plan a nice dinner. That would work best for us. What do you say?" With that honesty, they could have created a comfortable evening in front of the television like Jennifer and Tom preferred that also included Mary.

There are subtleties that go into treating someone like part of the family, and many ways to do it. Leave a grocery list up on the refrigerator and mention, "I'm going to the store; make sure you write down what you need." Let your parent do the dishes or laundry, assuming they are able to do so.

One way to tell if you are viewing your housemate parent as a guest is by monitoring your feelings and word choice. Are you annoyed when your mother is always at the dinner table? How about when you come home from work and she is there? Do you feel relieved when your parent is out and say to yourself, "Oh good, I can relax now"?

Treating your parent like a member of the family can be freeing for you as well. You won't have to wait until your parent leaves for the afternoon to relax; you can unwind while she is home. Ask for what you need. Remember that a lot of communication is unspoken, and your parent will instinctively know if you see her as an intrusion. You can work toward remedying this by reminding yourself of why you made the decision to move your parent in and set some boundaries and rules that can give you additional privacy if you need it.

Don't Avoid the Tough Stuff
Have the hard conversations right away, or as soon as issues arise. It won't be easy, but it is more important to have the

difficult conversation than to build and harbor resentment. Do not assume your parent can determine what you need and want. Remember that your parent will probably feel displaced and more needy than usual. Find ways to lovingly talk to her about what you need. For example: "Mary, we're just not used to another adult around when we come home from work when we are unwinding. We're not trying to be rude. We love you and enjoy your company, but when we come home from work, we are just so fried that sometimes we're not the most conversational people—but it has nothing to do with you. We just need a little alone time. Thanks so much for understanding."

Look forward to living together for the long haul. Lamenting how things used to be is a waste of your energy and will lead to frustration. Accept the new living arrangement and focus on making it work. Do you feel like you are waiting for something? Do you feel tense? These are signs that you may still see the living arrangement as temporary. Remind yourself that it is permanent. See the reference section of this book for resources to help work through the difficulties in caring for an elderly parent.

Leave Resentment at the Door

Some families feel like they have no choice but to move a parent in with them. Even if that is the case, once you have accepted the responsibility, let go of the resentment you may feel. Resentment will make it difficult to make the move work. Acceptance will allow you to create a new living scenario that works well for all of the family members. Watch out for signs that you are clinging to feelings of resentment. Are you short with your parent? Impatient? If so, working on acceptance may help. Unfortunately, acceptance is not a one-time decision; it is a decision that requires focus and commitment to maintain.

Be Sensitive when Mom Seems Worried about Intruding

The transition from independent living to living with a grown child is difficult for your parent (see Chapter 9). Be sensitive if your parent seems tentative or uncomfortable, or even unsure of how much help to offer or how to contribute to the household. Notice if your parent apologizes too much: "I'm sorry, am I bothering you?" "I'm sorry, I just got myself a bowl of cereal and I haven't had a chance to wash my dish." "I'm sorry; I was just trying to help." "I'm sorry, I don't mean to intrude."

Is your parent nervous or trying too hard to fit in or to avoid disrupting the family? Is your parent afraid you're going to kick her out, leaving her with nowhere to go if she doesn't "behave"? Help her out and remind her, "We want you here. We love you, and you are part of the family." Your parent may feel stressed out or even become depressed if she feels rejected. A major sign to look for is whether she spends too much time in the bedroom. If so, invite her to join you. Make sure your parent knows she is wanted and isn't a bother.

Physical Adjustments

As we touched upon in the previous chapter, it's very important to welcome your parent's possessions in the house. Most people take comfort in their surroundings, especially if their possessions have sentimental value. Make an effort to put some of your parent's cherished items not only in his room, but also spread throughout the house. If Grandpa usually sits in the old arm chair in the living room, place his favorite picture in his line of vision. Small gestures go a long way. You don't need to redecorate to accommodate your father-in-law's taste, but adding a few of his possessions could give him comfort, and it would be a nice step toward integrating him into the family.

Consider ways you could arrange the surroundings to make your parent feel at home. For example, stock the kitchen with your dad's favorite food or coffee. Ask for help around the house to show him that he is needed. Have him participate in family routines such as kitchen duties. Make room in the driveway for his car. Have him read to your first grader. Make sure his room is comfortable in every way.

Be sure to include your parent's routines into your schedule. No one wants to feel like a burden. If your dad has to remind you the first Saturday of every month that he has his poker night and he is met with "I forgot, I was planning dinner with Emily. That's okay, I can cancel . . ." he will feel like he is imposing or that he is a burden or afterthought. Instead, if you agree to take him, make sure you write it in your calendar each month so he will feel important to you. Bring up poker night a couple days before to show him that you are thinking of him.

Lessons Learned

Inviting your parent into your home is a generous and loving gesture. However, a common trap for those making that move is similar to the trap that some brides fall into. They get so caught up in the planning, preparation, and excitement about the wedding that they aren't thinking about what it will mean to be married. Jennifer and Tom had this same experience when planning the details of the move. They hadn't thought much past the details of selling the house, the construction of the addition, and the delays so they hadn't worked out the interpersonal details. It was all fine, until Jennifer looked up, saw her mother-in-law on the sofa, and it dawned on her—the move was permanent. Mary wasn't leaving. Finally, Jennifer got it.

The shock had nothing to do with Mary and the type of guest, mother, or mother-in-law she was. Everyone loved her—they all got along unusually well. In fact, Mary often referred to Jennifer as her favorite daughter. And Jennifer thought of Mary as a second mother. However, regardless of how well adults get along on vacations or short-term visits, never underestimate the potential difficulties when adults move in together. Just think of the adjustments you may have made when you first got married or when your children grew up and turned into teenagers! Difficulties don't always have to do with arguments or clashing personalities; sometimes the difficulties are more abstract and have to do with family privacy and disrupted routines (see Chapter 10).

When it comes right down to it, the families we interviewed that felt the move was successful and had fewest bumps along the way had several similarities in attitude, preparation, and patience. Interestingly, this also held true for families not just moving a parent in who was healthy and relatively independent, but ones who had medical issues requiring care from the adult children as well. Their attitude was open and they had a willingness to accept the housemate parent as a member of the family. They had prepared for the changes in the family dynamic and routines. Often, successful families recognized that there would be changes, even if they couldn't predict them. Most of all, they had patience. Patience through arguments, mistakes, missed cues, and inadvertently hurt feelings, for themselves, and for all of the unexpected happenings.

chapter 8

creating and maintaining family harmony

PEOPLE WITH DIFFICULT or stubborn personalities will probably continue to be stubborn or difficult as they age. They may
even become more difficult. To make the new living arrangement work, it is crucial that you take control of the aspects
of the relationship that are in your control—your thoughts,
behaviors, and feelings. It is equally important to realize
where you have little or no control—your parent's thoughts,
behaviors, and feelings.

It is possible that if you change your reaction to your
parent's difficult personality, she may soften and be open to
healthy and appropriate ways to deal with fear, anxiety, loneliness, or depression. In many cases, especially with seniors, the
difficulty stems from fear or feelings of powerlessness. While
that doesn't make it easier to deal with the person exhibiting
the behavior, that insight may trigger compassion. You may
feel resentful that you are responsible for restoring harmony
in your home, especially if your parent has behaved poorly.
Remember, you made a choice to move her in, and it will be
your action that gives the move the best chance of working.

Stop Wishing—and Start Doing

If you decide to live with your difficult parent and you want to make the arrangement work, eliminate the following wishes from your mind:

I wish my parent would stop:
- Trying to manipulate me
- Trying to control me
- Making me feel guilty
- Needing to be right
- Defending his point of view
- Criticizing
- Being selfish
- Giving advice
- Telling me what to wear
- Blaming me
- Being preoccupied with his own needs and wants
- Always being around
- Looking for magical cures
- Nagging
- Rejecting me
- Micromanaging
- Telling the same story over and over
- Being so pessimistic
- Rejecting my help
- Being stubborn about taking medicine and seeing doctors

Wishing something would change perpetuates the belief that you have no control over your situation. Each time you think, "I just wish my parent would . . . " you confirm your helplessness. You subconsciously acknowledge that your life and peace of mind are at the mercy of your parent; or worse, you begin silently waiting for your parent to pass away just so you can find peace. That old wish list also keeps you stuck in the unhealed adult-child role, making it much more difficult for you to care for yourself, your own family, and your aging parent. Abdicating your power or your responsibility for your own happiness assures that the living arrangement will fail. Take control of your life, your thoughts, your peace of mind, and give the new family unit a chance to succeed.

Add the following actions to your to-do list.

Accept Your Parent as He Is

Accept that your parent will not change; but of course, allow for the possibility that he will. Hoping your parent will change or harboring anger wastes your mental energy and sends the message that your parent holds the key to your family's happiness, which, of course, isn't true. Stop and remind yourself that you are involved in a relationship with your parent and that all relationships have at least two people who are responsible for the dynamic.

Remember that you only have control over your part of the relationship; you do not have any control over what your parent thinks, says, or does. Decide to change the part of your relationship that you control—your reaction to your parent. Stop yourself when you hear yourself saying, "I wish Dad would change." Change that thought into, "How can I lovingly react to Dad's difficult personality?" This is easier said than done. Be patient with yourself and keep trying—you'll get there.

Stop Punishing and Blaming Your Parent for the Past

If you are actively punishing your parent (this includes big gestures such as avoiding conversation or excluding him from family activities as well as small ones like eye rolling), you are not only preventing family harmony, you are also teaching your children a negative lesson. Remember that your children model your example. They see how you treat your parents and they are quite likely to treat you and other people that same way. In addition, you are creating unfavorable emotions that make it difficult for you to relate lovingly toward your spouse, children, and friends. Negative emotions are contagious and can poison an entire family.

As head of the house, you set the tone for your family. Decide what message you would like to give. You may never force your parent to see the error of his ways, but Dad, just like all of us, is less likely to be disruptive when he is treated with respect. How you treat Dad is a statement of the type of person you are, not the type of person he is or has been.

Act from the Adult Role

One of your many goals when moving your parent into your home is to maintain family harmony. Responding to your parent as you did when you were a child will not preserve your role as head of the house, nor will it show your children a generous and gracious way to behave during adversity. Most importantly, reacting to your parent as you did when you were a child will create so much stress that it will be difficult for you to maintain your marriage or sanity. If you change the way you relate to your parent, the relationship will change. Stand firm in who you are and how you want to treat others. This will preserve your home life, happiness, and sanity.

Set Boundaries

Set boundaries and stick to them, just as you must when you raise children. Prioritize your family and yourself, not your parent's demands. This is not to say that your parent's needs are not a top priority; they are. However, your parent's demands may not be. A confusing part of caring for a parent with a difficult personality is to identify where your responsibilities begin and where they end. Many difficult people attempt to make others responsible for their own well-being, happiness, and care while abdicating personal responsibility. If your parent has used these manipulative tactics since you were young, you may feel guilty about setting boundaries. Accept your limitation and your own family obligations. Your responsibility to your parent does not supersede your responsibility to your children, spouse, and yourself, regardless of what Dad wants you to think. You will take care of your parent, but not at the expense of your own family. A selfish parent may continue to ask you for more and more, as long as you are willing to comply. Set a boundary and show Dad what you are willing and not willing to do.

Changing long-standing relationships is difficult to do. Consider getting support or help in making these changes. See the reference section of this book for resources on understanding and healing relationships.

Don't Become a Difficult Person Yourself

Regardless of your childhood or the type of parents you had, you are now an adult and you can choose how you want to live, form relationships, and raise your children. Your parents may have shaped your past and even some of your ingrained beliefs about yourself, but your future is in your own hands.

Don't spend your life holding onto anger, resentment, blame, and bitterness. Look in the reference section of this book for resources for outgrowing a difficult childhood, coping with a difficult or narcissistic parent, and stepping into your own power, beyond the grasp of the unhealed people around you.

ONE FAMILY'S EXPERIENCE *Miranda and Celeste*

Miranda and Celeste had a difficult father. They learned the hard way that they were in control of their own harmony, not their father, Seymour.

Miranda and Celeste, the two youngest of six daughters, decided to work together to care for their elderly father, Seymour. Their father wasn't sick, but since his stroke he was less mobile and had permanent short-term memory loss. He was also insulin dependent due to his diabetes. Left to himself, Seymour would forget to take his medication, or take it multiple times in one day; it was unsafe for him to live on his own. Neither Celeste nor Miranda jumped at the chance to take him in. They both worked hard to create nice lives for themselves, and felt that their father was a disruptive influence.

Miranda and Celeste searched for any care solution for their father, short of moving him into either of their homes. After they exhausted all alternatives, Miranda and Celeste finally decided Seymour would move in with one of them.

Seymour didn't want to leave Towson, Maryland, where he lived his entire life, to move in with Celeste who had a large home in the country. Instead, he wanted to live with his youngest daughter, Miranda, who lived close by. After many arguments, Seymour moved into Miranda's small, three-bedroom, one and a half-bathroom house. It was a tight fit. However, within a few weeks the newly formed unit—Miranda, her husband Dan their son Jack, and Seymour—began to gel. Miranda and Dan felt they had no choice but to move Seymour in with them, yet were pleasantly surprised at how well they all settled into the new arrangement. Actually, they felt fairly good about it, especially after they found Ellen, a loving experienced home health aide. Her services cost about $675 per week, but she was worth it. She had no problem standing up to his demanding personality. All in all, she did a great job, and even Seymour seemed to like her.

One month into the arrangement, Ellen called in sick. Miranda decided to handle it the same way she would if her child was sent home from school with a sore throat—she took the day off from work. Her father was thrilled to have Miranda take care of him. Miranda stayed home with her father for two days, and finally on the third day Ellen was back to work. Seymour wasn't happy about it.

Two weeks later, Seymour called Miranda at work and said, "I fired Ellen. She was terrible. You have to take care of me." That wasn't an option for Miranda, so she immediately began trying to replace Ellen (who, in her mind, was perfect for the job). The home health agency sent a slew of capable aides to help out. Seymour disliked everyone who came in. It was clear that Seymour had his mind set on Miranda as his caretaker. Miranda and Dan put interim caretakers in place, but Seymour seemed fixated on his daughter and called her at work several times a day with "emergencies." He would become irate when she didn't immediately return his calls. In frustration, Seymour would tell her and other family members that she was a bad daughter and didn't care about him. Miranda still had Celeste, but that really didn't ease her burden.

No matter how carefully Miranda tried to plan, the unexpected interruption or problem seemed to happen, some of which were Seymour's doing, some not. Emotionally exhausted by it all, Miranda became suspicious and could no longer tell if Seymour's problems and ailments were real or if he was trying to manipulate her. At times it was hard for her to remember that her father truly did need help, because she was overwhelmed and resentful. Her life was no longer her own. To make matters worse, she and Dan were fighting from all the stress. It was Miranda's worst nightmare.

That's how it began. Miranda took her new role as care-taker very seriously and did everything right: she made a plan; she made her house safe by increasing the lighting and tacking down any loose carpets; she learned about her father's condition and needs; made a schedule of doctor appointments; learned how to test blood sugar and administer insulin; arranged for capable, caring home health care; and even organized Seymour's finances. With all her care and planning, what went wrong? Personalities, fears, needs, stress, aging with its ensuing complications, unrealistic expectations, the unexpected, and a difficult parent . . . that's what went wrong.

Seymour has a difficult personality and always has; this isn't new. However, he was aging and did have legitimate needs. As long as Miranda was angry with him and operating from the unhealed adult-child mode, there was no way to set clear boundaries, see the situation clearly, and make strong productive decisions that could help him. In fact some of his requests and concerns were justified, but she immediately assumed he was always trying to control her, making it impossible to see when he did have a legitimate concern.

Miranda was intimidated by her father and stood in a defensive posture waiting for him to try to bully and manipulate her. She felt stuck between wanting to help him and wanting to run away. Seymour was afraid of being alone and felt rejected, hurt, and bewildered that Miranda didn't want to devote her life to him. His old method of manipulating had always worked with her in the past and he couldn't figure out why it wasn't working now.

It may seem as though Seymour was the one creating all the problems; the truth is, Miranda was adding to the mix because she rarely gave her father clear information. She was nervous about setting defined boundaries and telling him that she was not going to quit her job and take care of him. Instead, when new aides showed up, Miranda would make herself unavailable and was often short or irritated in her conversations with him. They were both frustrated.

Miranda needed to step into the adult role, take responsibility for her feelings and desires, give her Dad non-negotiable information, and most importantly, follow through with her rules. If not, she was essentially telling Seymour that her definitive stance was simply the beginning of a negotiation, instead of a bottom-line statement. She finally sat down with Seymour and told him, honestly and lovingly, "Dad, I love you and will do what I can to make sure you are safe and happy. This is why we moved you in with us. I will not quit my job. I will not be your full-time caretaker. I will help you find an aide that you like, but I will not be that aide. When you call me at work, I will get back to you as soon as I can. It may not be right away, but I will always call you back. If it is an emergency, call 911."

This made an enormous difference to both of them. Knowing that she was clear and getting her own needs met made it easier for Miranda to really listen to her father's concerns and have an adult conversation. Feeling confident that she wouldn't allow herself to be forced into a position she didn't want to be in made it that much easier for her to be in a relationship with her dad. Feeling safe herself, she could then see her father's fear. The good news was that when Miranda stepped out of the adult-child role and into the adult role, she could support him. He felt seen and heard; he felt less rejected and therefore was less demanding. Seymour still had a difficult personality, but Miranda didn't feel as victimized by it. When Miranda stopped playing into the old roles, the house was less stressful and the new dynamic worked for all of them. The power struggle was slowly ebbing, and though it took some time, they all began to relax into the new living arrangement.

Lessons Learned

If you are caring for a difficult elderly parent, maintaining your adult self with your parent will be a challenge at times. Remind yourself that you are not only living your adult role for your parent, but for your children and spouse as well. If you are always on edge, treating your children and spouse with patience and love becomes difficult. Treat your parent the way you would ultimately want to be treated by your children.

Your parent has lost the opportunity to parent you the way you would have liked. But it is not too late to take responsibility for your own life and how you want to impact your own children. Do not be a replica of your parent. Be your best self and act from a loving and kind place, whether or not you feel your parent deserves it. This is the goal and the motivation for you to see your parent through loving eyes, which will have far-reaching implications for you and your entire family.

chapter 9

your parent's perspective

As THE OLD ADAGE says, "No matter how flat the pancake, there are always two sides." Remember that your parent has an entirely different perspective about moving into your home than you have. In addition, the person living with you didn't become old in one day. She grew up; had expectations, hopes and dreams; and lived life as best she could—just like you. It is unlikely that this old person, your parent, ever expected or wanted to end up in a situation where she couldn't take care of herself. This person deserves understanding and compassion, just as we all do.

When your parent moves in with you your life changes; when your parent moves in with you her life changes much more. Your parent may move in for any number of reasons, many of which are not good:

- Death of a spouse
- Failing health
- Depression
- Mental deterioration

- Financial difficulties
- Loneliness
- Frailty
- Incompetence

Difficult behavior is usually a sign of fear, anxiety, hopelessness, depression, insecurity, self-doubt, a reaction to pain, or to a medical condition. Aggression, combativeness, and abusiveness often accompany strokes or forms of dementia. If your parent's behavior seems unreasonable, ask yourself, "Is Mom reacting to a difficult situation? Is she afraid?" It is important when dealing with an elderly parent to remember the person she used to be. No matter how difficult an adjustment for you and your family, it is probably more difficult for your parent.

The many families who have moved parents in with them and considered it successful found ways to show compassion and forgiveness and to ignore some difficult behavior, as they recognized the emotional turmoil their parent was experiencing. Consider the following to help your parent transition into this new living arrangement.

Make Sure the Time Is Right to Move Your Parent

Before moving your parent into your home, make sure the timing is right. Many adult children, anxious to care for their parent, rush to make the move at the onset of an illness or death of a spouse. The general rule of thumb is to keep your parent in his own home for as long as safely possible, even if that means you must hire a home health worker for extra support. Experts believe that keeping life as normal as possible for your parent can preserve and maintain psychological and emotional well-being. One's own home offers a great deal of comfort, especially in time of loss and change.

Commonly, the older generations have attached a stigma to moving out of their homes and into assisted living facilities, as they tend to see them in the same light as nursing homes—a place where one goes to die. Of course this isn't true, but there may still be end-of-life thoughts if they are pressured or convinced to leave their homes. You may think, "Moving into my home is not the same as moving into an old folk's home. This is different; he will like living with us." That may be true, but the elderly parent may also see the move into your home as an end-of-life decision and feel powerless and defeated. This is exactly what happened with Elizabeth.

ONE FAMILY'S EXPERIENCE *Elizabeth*

I don't remember the exact moment I became invisible. I can't put my finger on the day that I became someone to manage as opposed to someone enjoyable to be with, to visit, to share thoughts and ideas with. I think it started six months after I buried my husband, the man with whom I had just celebrated my sixtieth wedding anniversary. I see now that the day of his funeral was a foreshadowing of things to come, but I had no idea at the time. It happened after the service when my four children, huddled together, started planning. Planning what? I later discovered—the best way to "manage Mom." I never thought of myself as someone who needed to be managed. My children, however, who loved me a great deal, had their own thoughts about it.

Weeks after the funeral, my youngest son decided that it was all too much for me and he would help out: "Don't worry Mom; I'll take care of you." It sounded nice, and I felt comforted. He offered to handle my finances and oversee some much-needed repairs on my home. It was sweet and generous of him, but it turned out to be a slippery slope. A short time later I found myself making out a will and signing an array of legal documents, half of which were a mystery to me. I just signed "Mrs. Elizabeth Baker" where my son told me to sign. I was overwhelmed, and maybe even a little depressed by it. I didn't want to think about who gets my china and my wedding ring. It was too much. With my son's gentle encouragement, I got my affairs in order.

A few months later my daughter, Janine, sat me down for a serious talk. "Mom, you haven't been taking care of yourself or the house. You seem confused sometimes, and you definitely shouldn't be driving. You've missed doctor's appointments, and I am worried about you." My explanations and defense about why I missed appointments were useless—she had made up her mind and didn't want to hear my side of the story. She then told me she was selling my car and suggested (very strongly, I might add) that I move in with her.

Initially I didn't want to leave my home. I wasn't ready, but she was persistent. I don't remember the details of how I came to agree with her. I just remember sitting at my breakfast table, by myself, having a cup of coffee. Over the last sixty years I had never made coffee for one. I thought, "This is no way to live. I'm sure Janine could use a little help around the house anyway." I thought it might be nice to be part of a family again. I can help cook dinner, and clean, and decorate for holidays. I agreed, I moved, but it didn't quite work out the way I had envisioned.

Somewhere in the back of my mind, I thought I might be co-mother of the house again. That wasn't very realistic.

The hardest parts of the new living arrangement for me were having all my things stuffed into one room as well as trying to work myself into their lives. I didn't want to interfere with my daughter's routines or how she handles her own house. My advice and input was clearly unwelcome. I could feel Janine bristle when I would mention more efficient ways to organize the kitchen cabinets or to sort laundry. It wasn't as though I didn't have experience running a household; but still, I tried to stay out of the way. Their lives were active and busy, and it all seemed to swirl around me.

I wasn't unhappy, but I just felt out of place. I knew how to be woman of the house—I didn't know how to be Grandma on the periphery. I couldn't even spoil my grandchildren the way I used to. Offering an extra cookie or gift when they came to my house for a visit was one thing, but that extra cookie or concession, on a daily basis, was undermining my daughter and son-in-law's authority while I was living under their roof. It was a real adjustment.

It all finally hit me one night at dinner. Janine made a beautiful meal of chicken marsala. I don't care for chicken; never have. So I ate salad and soup, and took just enough of chicken to appear polite. My daughter asked me, "What's wrong, Mom? Not hungry?" I told her I had a big lunch since I wouldn't expect her to change her menus for me. She replied, "Eat it; you'll like it. Go ahead, eat it." And she put a big piece on my plate and just watched me and waited. "Taste it," she coaxed. I took a piece of chicken and slowly chewed. I felt sad and powerless. I lost my husband, my home, my independence, and life as I had known it, and now, I even lost my right to dislike chicken.

By any standards, Elizabeth was fortunate; she was relatively healthy and surrounded by loving children who wanted to take care of her. However, there were two problems. The first was that Janine didn't realize Elizabeth wasn't ready to leave her home, and medically didn't have to. Maybe Elizabeth was a little forgetful. Maybe she needed a little more supervision in getting to doctor appointments or to the hairdresser, but she didn't need to give up her home and life just yet. Remaining in the home maintains normalcy, routines, and a sense of purpose. A better solution than moving Elizabeth out of her home just months after her husband's death would have been to have an aide come and visit and take her to appointments or to help her with household chores. This would have given Elizabeth time to transition into her life without her husband. Moving out of the house she lived in for sixty years just created more unnecessary loss. Janine wanted to care for her mother, but the move was premature and may not have been necessary.

The next problem began immediately after the move took place. Janine stopped treating Elizabeth as an adult—someone with likes and dislikes, opinions, and with something valuable to contribute to the household. Janine started treating her mom as someone for whom she was responsible—almost a child—rather than as her mother who had once been the competent, sassy orchestrator of all that happened under the Baker's busy roof.

As soon as Elizabeth moved in with Janine and her family, she sensed her relegation in role. She hated it. She felt useless and invisible. She wasn't losing her hearing; she hadn't lost IQ points. So why were people talking to her loudly and slowly? She couldn't figure it out. At dinner when everyone was chatting away about their day, Elizabeth felt skipped over. "Don't

I have something worthwhile to share? Have I no wisdom left? Do I matter at all?" Every now and then, Janine would say, "Mom, what do you think?" But Elizabeth didn't hear any sincerity in the question. It was more a feeble attempt to include her. "I used to be smart, funny, and interesting. I'm not so sure anymore. Using my favorite Brendan Sullivan analogy, I feel like I have turned into a potted plant."

Conversely, there are times when your parent can no longer safely live alone and must change his living arrangement immediately. This was the case with Art.

ONE FAMILY'S EXPERIENCE *Art*

Eighty-five-year-old Art lived alone. His was quite independent and his brain was still sharp—he drove, he shopped, took care of himself, the house, and his birds, Eddie and Gus. Then, like falling dominoes, Art had one medical problem after another. It started after he had contracted pneumonia. While in the hospital, he developed a secondary infection and swelling in his legs. And then, to top it all off, he had a series of small strokes that left him confused and dizzy. In one week he went from independent and life of the party to a frightened, slightly disoriented old man. As he described it, his body turned against him.

Art didn't have much family, but was close to his niece, Danielle. Danielle and Art had always taken care of each other so naturally, Danielle visited Art every day while he was in the hospital and during his recovery in the rehab facility. A week before his impending release, Art was annoyed to find that his doctors wanted to include Danielle in every conversation. However, when the doctors and nurses were talking to Art, he had a hard time remembering things, and during the conversations he had a difficult time understanding what they were saying. There were many important decisions to be made about Art's care and prognosis. The doctors wanted to make sure Art had family present to participate in the conversations as well as to carry out the future plans.

While Art was still in rehab, Danielle wanted to make sure her Uncle Art understood what the doctors had prescribed, so she went through each medication and it's purpose and how often he needed to take it. She also reiterated the doctor's concern about Art's birds as well as his living arrangement. Art became enraged and verbally abusive: "Those idiot doctors don't know what they are talking about. I am just fine. I want to go back home, and like hell I'm getting rid of my birds." He raged on. Art even accused Danielle of not caring or taking the time to visit. Danielle was hurt by his accusations and very upset. She didn't know how to talk to her uncle and how to get through to him that it wasn't safe for him to live alone, and that the birds and their droppings were actually detrimental to his health. In Danielle's mind, Art was acting irrationally. He was combative with the nurses, the doctors, and her. This just wasn't like him.

However, Art wasn't trying to be difficult; he was scared. For the first time in his life, he felt out of control. He was dizzy and confused, and worse, people were telling him things that didn't make sense or that he didn't remember. Some doctor was telling him he couldn't live in his own house or keep his beloved birds. The nurse was telling him he had already eaten dinner, when he couldn't remember having done so. His only ally was his niece, and she was never around—or so he thought. He was at his wit's end.

Danielle looked for an assisted living facility where her uncle could live for at least temporary supervised housing. Art felt Danielle was trying to abandon him, and pawn him off on some nursing home where he would be left to die. He refused to move. He said he was going home, and that was it: "I can take care of myself, I always have." As an interim solution, Danielle suggested that Art consider staying with her until he felt better. That seemed to be a good solution, but then Art brought up the birds. Danielle thought they were noisy, dirty, and smelly, not to mention bad for Art's lungs. To make matters worse, Art refused to keep them in cages and let them fly free, leaving bird droppings everywhere. He was adamant that the birds would get depressed if they were locked up. He wouldn't do that to his loyal companions.

Danielle couldn't believe how unreasonable her uncle was being. He couldn't live alone and he just couldn't seem to get that through his head. Art, on the other hand, felt that Danielle was being unreasonable: "My birds are not trash. They have been loyal friends and good company. I don't want to upset them with change."

They argued back and forth. Art finally agreed to stay with Danielle until he got better, and to keep Eddie and Gus locked in the guest room. Danielle knew that Art was never going to get better, but at least she got him out of his house: "Boy, Uncle Art has turned into such a grouch."

Was Art grouchy? Probably. He had a lot to be angry about. One day he was living his life, making his own decisions, caring for his birds, and the next day he is told he had a conversation that he can't remember having, he can't go back to his home, and he has to give up his long-time companions. Put yourself in his shoes—you'd be grouchy, too.

When you have a parent or a loved one who, like Art, has always been independent and firmly rooted in routine, it can be devastating for him to hear that he isn't okay anymore. From

Art's perspective, he was fine. He didn't realize the strokes left him impaired. He was outraged to hear doctors telling him he could no longer do the things he had done his entire life. Danielle made matters worse by becoming impatient and annoyed at her uncle's inability to "get with the program."

Consider Your Parent's Feelings

The reality of Art's situation is heartbreaking. Unfortunately, it is still a reality for many aging people. You can't change that reality for your parent, but you can help her through the transition by remaining compassionate and loving. If you find yourself feeling impatient or annoyed with your parent, remind yourself that she may be feeling some or all of the following:

- Panicked about failing health and memory loss
- Sad about the prospect of giving up her home
- Worried about what will become of her
- Lonely, far from friends, grieving the loss of a spouse, home alone
- That her needs are infringing on the family
- As though she is being treated like a child
- Isolated and as though she does not have a life
- Dependent because she can no longer drive
- Embarrassed by medical needs
- Ashamed of money issues
- Nervous about disturbing your routine

Art was faced with a disastrous situation through no fault of his own. He deserved understanding and patience.

Both Elizabeth and Art resented being managed. They had both been strong, independent people. Your parent probably had a full and active life, too. Remember to treat your parent as a person, not as a responsibility. When you treat your parent as a responsibility, rather than as a person with thoughts, feelings, and emotions, you may inadvertently neglect to make her part of your family dynamic. Treating your parent like an added burden will have a detrimental effect on her, and chances are very good that she will pick up on your feelings. This is what happened between Janine and Elizabeth. It is true that caring for an elderly parent, especially when illness is involved, is like a job; however, you can take care of your parent and still treat her as you would a member of the family. Don't make Janine's mistake and treat your parent like a child (regardless of her limitations), but rather as someone who deserves your respect and care.

Allow Your Parent to Contribute to the Household

One way to make your moved-in parent feel like a member of the family is to allow her to contribute to the household. Even if your parent is financially limited, she still may have the ability to offer something valuable. Take advantage of that ability. It will bolster self-esteem and give her something to do as well as offer a natural way for her to fit in.

Don't limit your thoughts to money contributions. Dog walking, packing lunches, baby sitting, cooking, dinner cleanup, laundry folding, sewing, and helping with homework are just a few ways a parent can contribute. Maybe she can't do these things all the time, but maybe there is something else she can do to contribute that you have forgotten. Keep your eyes open to what she might be able to do to help. What does your parent like to do? Find a way to let her do it; who knows, you might even learn something.

In Art's case, he was becoming frail and his memory was spotty. However, he loved to cook. Danielle found him to be disruptive in the kitchen during dinner, as he wanted to put canned cream of mushroom soup over every dish; however, he turned out to be a big help in the morning when she was getting her children's lunches packed. He made great peanut butter and jelly sandwiches and looked forward to helping out.

In Elizabeth's case, she found herself looking in from the outside. She felt she had nothing to say or contribute to the household. Finally, Janine came up with a plan that suited the entire family. She put her mom in charge of the family calendar.

Organizing the family's busy schedule was no small feat; Elizabeth was excited to take on the job. Every day after school, the three kids would tell their grandmother what activities were coming up in their schedules—soccer practice, ballet lessons, a sleepover. In addition, Elizabeth would record hairdresser and doctor appointments, birthdays, and upcoming tests and quizzes. She even recorded when Jeff's car was due for an oil change. Everything went on the big calendar that Janine brought home. This process served many purposes, such as:

- It kept the family organized.
- It encouraged each child to have a meaningful conversation with their grandmother—they had a real reason to share their day and schedule.
- It gave Elizabeth something important to do for the family and kept her in the loop on activities.

- It helped Elizabeth once again feel like the orchestrator of events, which she loved.
- It gave Elizabeth a way to talk about what was on her agenda.
- Elizabeth was able to participate in family discussions and ask the right questions: "How do you think you did on the quiz? How was soccer practice?"
- The calendar job made sure that Elizabeth had everyone's birthdays and anniversaries written down. She was forgetful, so it also gave her comfort to have important dates down on paper, and that she was the one to help people remember. It gave her a purpose.
- Elizabeth became the go-to person for scheduling, and was now in the family loop.

After the initiation of the family calendar, Elizabeth no longer felt like someone who was being managed or taken care of, but a member of the household. A happy Elizabeth made for a happy Janine and a happy family.

Help Your Parent Retain Meaning in His Life

Many adults reaching retirement age are nervous about taking the step to leave their careers behind. This is true even for many who have never particularly loved their jobs. The main reason? They are faced with the question, "What am I going to do with myself?" Those who have hobbies or a rich social life or a spouse with whom they have travel plans or a dream of biking across Europe or who have been waiting to do community service are less reticent about retirement. For the rest of the population, it can be a scary thought.

In addition to full-time work, many people have hours of activity surrounding their homes: cleaning, organizing, gardening, entertaining, visiting neighbors, and keeping up with repairs. What happens when a spouse passes away or health begins to deteriorate and the person sells their home and moves away from friends? Everyone needs something that gets them up in the morning and inspires them throughout the day. Everyone needs something of relevance that occupies the mind. A sense of purpose is crucial for every individual to keep from falling into depression or losing his or her passion for life.

Talk to your parent and find out what activities would reawaken joy and anticipation. Playing cards at the local senior center is not for everyone. Activities merely for the sake of filling up time may not restore a sense of purpose and enthusiasm in your parent's life. Work together to find something that has meaning to him; the goal is to help bring joy back into your parent's life, not to merely plant him somewhere.

Art derived most of his joy from taking care of his birds. It's true that letting them freely fly around wasn't the best decision for Art's physical health, but he needed his birds for his emotional health. Danielle initially agreed to let the birds stay in the guest room, but that didn't work very well. Art wouldn't keep the birds in the cage, and Danielle was becoming more upset about the mess. Over time, as Art got comfortable staying with Danielle, he permanently moved in. As a concession, Danielle and her husband sectioned off a part of the basement where the birds could fly free and Art could sit and watch them. That was all he wanted—a bit of life as he had known it.

That is all anyone really wants—for life to feel normal. Erin and Dan found a wonderful way for Jill's mother to hold on to her favorite hobby after she moved in with them.

ONE FAMILY'S EXPERIENCE *Erin and Dan*

Dan and his wife Jill lived in a beautiful country home with a large backyard. Three years prior, Erin, Jill's mother, moved in with them. Every spring and summer, Erin would sit on the back porch and just watch as Dan mowed, weeded, and cared for the lawn and garden. It occurred to Dan that Erin loved to garden and maybe she'd like to help him. He invited her to join him, but she declined. Confused, Dan spoke to Jill about the matter. Jill reminded him that her mother had her own garden and her own way of doing things. Dan finally understood that Erin didn't want to help him with his garden, she missed having her own. So Dan wrote up an official-looking deed to the backyard. It spelled out that she was granted ownership and was responsible from that day on for beautifying the land, without their interference. He said, with her permission, that he would still mow the lawn. Dan was pleased to do that for his mother-in-law, and she was truly happy in return.

Treat Your Parent with Respect

Respecting and honoring your parent is always important, but this attitude and approach becomes crucial when he moves into your home. There are many ways to respect your parent: You can do so with words or gestures; you can also show respect by honoring the things he values. If your parent has an ugly, chipped bowling trophy that means the world to him, your inclination may be to hide it away because it doesn't go with your décor. It would be respectful and generous of you to put it in the den or living room so he can catch a glimpse of it every now and then.

If your parent has a particular ritual that is important, think about incorporating it into your family routine, even if it doesn't hold the same importance to you. Brenda and Barbara found a way to compromise so that Barbara felt like she was a true member of the family.

ONE FAMILY'S EXPERIENCE *Brenda and Barbara*

Brenda was raised Jewish, but didn't continue with the practices once she started her own family. It wasn't a conscious decision; it just seemed to happen over the years. When Barbara, Brenda's mother, moved in, she wanted to bring many of the old traditions back into her daughter's home. Every Friday night, the traditional celebration of the Sabbath, Barbara reminded the family over dinner that she lit the Sabbath candles every Friday night for the last seventy-five years—until now. After a couple of months, Brenda and her husband got the not-so-subtle hint that this ritual would be meaningful for Barbara.

The next Friday night, Brenda brought out Barbara's Sabbath candles and invited her to light them and say the blessing. Barbara was so happy she cried. The entire ceremony lasted under three minutes, but brought Barbara great joy. She felt loved and respected, as she was able to share something very important to her with her grandchildren. Later on, Brenda also admitted it was nice to introduce a tradition to her own children that she grew up with. It worked out beautifully for everyone.

Find Ways to Restore a Level of Independence

Loss of independence is one of the greatest frustrations for the elderly, next to deteriorating health. Isolation and loss of independence is a widespread concern. It may be true that your parent can no longer drive; however, there are ways to help restore at least a little independence. One family gave their father gift certificates to a taxi and limousine service. He didn't use them very often, but he knew if he wanted to go somewhere and didn't want to bother his son for a ride, he had the ability to do so. Just knowing he could meant a lot to him.

Not all families can afford the high cost of taxi services. And in areas without extensive public transportation, it isn't practical. There are many free and subsidized groups that offer transportation for the elderly. Look into the National Association of Area Agencies on Aging (*www.n4a.org*, 202-872-0888) for a listing of agencies local to you who may offer these services. In addition, call local senior centers, religious groups, and charitable organizations to see if they offer transportation or have some advice.

Most adults would prefer not to have to ask for help with simple tasks. They may eventually give up before asking for help. You can restore some sense of independence by creating workarounds. Many families purchase stair lifts, making it easier for their parent to independently go up and down stairs. Other families move their parent's bedroom as well as the laundry room to the main floor, making it easier for their parent to navigate the house. Those afflicted with arthritis may have a difficult time opening cans and jars. There are many inexpensive automatic jar openers that can make the task doable. For a parent who is uncomfortable using a gas stove, a hot plate or microwave is a great way to heat soup or water for tea or coffee. Many large grocery stores have delivery services. Set up an account and allow your parent to grocery shop by phone or online. There are many little ways to help your parent feel more independent.

Lessons Learned

Simply put, the move into your home is no picnic for your parent. She must say goodbye to a lifestyle, independence, homeownership, and status as the head of the house. However, with your help, the move into your home can add a wonderful dimension to all of your lives, including your parent's. It doesn't have to mark the end; it can also be the beginning of something meaningful. Compassion for the loss your parent may experience is key in making the transition work for everyone involved. And when your parent is happy, the transition is easier for all of you. Remember:

- Honor your parent for who she used to be and who she is now.
- Work to restore dignity and a sense of purpose and responsibility to your parent.
- Rid yourself of self-focus and complaints about the difficulty you are faced with.
- Take the time to talk to your parent about her past.
- Show compassion for your parent's illness, mental and emotional condition, and frailties.
- Seek to strengthen what qualities and competencies your parent still has.
- Value your parent's contribution to your household.
- Listen attentively.

- Support your parent and give her a safe place to discuss fears.
- See beyond difficult behavior for the underlying emotions.
- Put yourself in your parent's shoes; aging is a process everyone experiences.
- Be a role model for your own children, and treat your parents how you would like to be treated.
- Be patient and understanding.
- Forgive. Forgive your parent for who she was, is, and will become. Forgive yourself for your limitations. Forgive the unfairness of aging, and accept what is.

chapter 10
preserving core family unity

JANE, STEPHEN, AND THEIR TWO KIDS spent ten wonderful days in the Caribbean. The weather, hotel, food, and atmosphere were all perfect. They had a great time. Yet, by the end of the trip they were all looking forward to going home. When they finally arrived home to their modest three-bedroom house, they let out a sigh of relief as they relaxed into their favorite chairs with the old worn-out pillows. They felt at peace.

What is family unity? Family unity is comprised of all the elements that make your family cohesive. It occurs when familiar routines, dynamics, expectations, and relationships are respected and upheld—all of which contribute to the needs and well-being of each family member, in addition to the unit as a whole. Family unity also includes the comfort you feel just by being in your own house. Maintaining and achieving family unity is a delicate balance.

What makes you feel peaceful in your home? Is it the fact that you and your spouse bought it together? Decorated it with things that you love? Developed routines and had family experiences in it over the years? No one really knows for sure. The only thing for certain is that your home has a "feel," which you and your family created. This sense of security is a crucial element of family unity. So, what happens when your mother moves in and has her own routines, not to mention lots of antiques, which your spouse dislikes? What about when you come home from work and instead of the usual peace and quiet, you are greeted by an in-law wanting to make small talk? Maybe your teenage daughter is no longer comfortable bringing friends home after school because Grandpa, who moved in last summer, enjoys sitting in the living room in his stained undershirt and boxer shorts with the fan blowing on him.

These are just a few things that can disrupt family unity when an elderly parent moves in with you. The level of disruption has nothing to do with how you feel about your father-in-law, or how kind and considerate your mother is. Anyone joining an existing core family, especially another adult who is used to being in charge, will change the feel of the home. Just as adding an additional ingredient to a recipe will change the flavor of the meal; moving a parent into the family (with the long emotional history that comes with him) will change the dynamic of that core family unit.

These disruptions can't be ignored. If you sit back and hope they will work themselves out, you may be in for some difficult times. Ignoring the long-term importance of family unity and the importance of incorporating your aging parent into the existing patterns can wreak havoc on your core family, as well as alienate your parent.

Here's the bad news: There is no one-size-fits-all, permanent, one-time quick fix. There are no solutions. Here's the good news: There are ways to manage situations as they arise, making life more comfortable for everyone. Throughout the process of recreating family unity to include and consider the housemate parent, remind yourself that problem management is possible in any circumstance. When dealing with people, especially a live-in parent, management of problems is the goal. You wouldn't expect to go to the gym one time and be in shape for life, would you? There are rarely one-time fixes for personal relationships, either.

Your goal will be to restore unity while creating a new dynamic including your parent. Once you are aware of what can happen and embrace the notion that this new family dynamic will be in constant flux, you will then have a greater chance of adapting to situations as they arise and creating harmony for you and your family.

Family unity covers a broad range of emotions and experiences. There are many threats to family unity, such as disruption of parental rights, routines, privacy, and individual internal harmony.

Disruption of Parental Rights

One of your many jobs as a parent is to make sure your household rules are consistently enforced, strengthening children's sense of security and character as they mature. The process of creating and enforcing rules can be difficult enough, let alone when someone else interferes. This is not to say that developing a new healthy family dynamic including your parent isn't crucial; it is. However, in most cases you and your spouse (or you alone if you have a single parent household) will want sole parental rule. Here's what can happen during the adjustment period when a parent moves in with you.

ONE FAMILY'S EXPERIENCE *Allen*

My two boys—Harry, age four, and Sam, age nine—argue all the time. At this point, my wife and I almost expect it. However, Harry takes the arguments too far with an aggressive tone of voice and inappropriate language. We haven't figured out where this comes from—cartoons, kids at school, or even his older brother. Curse words have, nevertheless, seeped into Harry's vocabulary. My wife and I have been working diligently to rid him of this habit by showing zero tolerance. It was a family rule, and he would get a time-out if he disobeyed. Arguing is fine; disagreeing is fine; bad language is not fine—ever.

One Saturday afternoon, Harry and Sam were fighting and Harry began cursing. I scolded Harry, told him once again that he must never use bad language in school or at home or toward anyone. I brought Harry to the time-out room and told him he could come out after ten minutes, and then he would have to apologize to Sam. Harry was quite riled up from the fight and reprimand and could be heard crying throughout the house. My wife and I were talking about it when we noticed my mother, Sandra, sneaking upstairs with cookies to comfort Harry. I felt like cursing at this point: I am the father, I have the right to set rules in my own home, and I do not appreciate being undermined. I know my mother didn't mean harm, but she caused it.

Sandra didn't mean to upset anyone. She just couldn't stand to hear Harry crying. Unfortunately, her desire to comfort him threw Allen's right to teach and discipline his own child out the window. She inadvertently undermined his efforts and authority with his kids. In doing so, she created a major rift.

Just because Grandma is uncomfortable when her grandchild cries, or believes you are too strict or not strict enough or is judgmental about your parenting choices, doesn't give her the right to contribute to raising your children unless you say it is okay. However, just because it is your right doesn't mean, at times, your parent won't encroach.

Set Clear Boundaries

Get used to discussing your rules and boundaries. You'll probably also have to discuss the little things such as how the refrigerator is arranged or where the mail goes before it is opened or if your dog can have table scraps after a meal. As you learned in Chapter 4, it is best to think about potential issues and discuss them before your parent moves in to get everyone used to thinking about the new living situation before problems arise. Getting used to these types of discussions shows that bringing up problems and frustrations doesn't have to be a big deal. In this case, the family's problem went a little deeper than Sandra's need to step back and leave child disciplining to Allen and his wife. When Allen broached the cookie incident with his mother, Sandra told him that she was just "Grandma being Grandma." Allen then realized that comforting Harry was just the symptom of the problem.

Sandra used to baby sit once or twice a month. During those visits, she was free to spoil her grandchildren. She would let them have the extra cookie, watch TV before they did their homework, go to bed late, or partake in other indulgences. That was their relationship. It worked because she was the grandparent and had a peripheral family role. In fact, it was nice for everyone. Unfortunately, that role changed the moment she moved in with the family. The change in the Grandma role was a loss that she was having a difficult time adjusting to. Now, indulging her grandchildren seemed to undermine her son's authority, and she didn't want to do that.

She hadn't expected this shift, and hasn't figured out how to handle it yet.

Ultimately, Allen and Sandra came to an understanding. Sandra agreed to refrain from interjecting when Allen and his wife discipline their children. Allen agreed to let Sandra keep her traditional role as grandmother once or twice a month, when she could indulge her grandchildren in any way she chose. They designated times and events—a trip to the circus or going to the movies—so that clear boundaries were set when she could and could not spoil them. This made it easier for all of them. Balance was restored and a new family dynamic created.

Disruption of Routines

A sure-fire way to rattle a core family is to disrupt their routines. Over many years, you, your spouse, and your children have developed an elaborate pattern of habitual behavior. Routine includes everything from who cooks dinner to what kind of books the children read before bed to when each parent gets quiet time. These routines create expectations, comfort in the home, and strengthen the family unit.

Stan's story is typical of what can happen when a parent is introduced into a family unit without first considering family habits and routines.

ONE FAMILY'S EXPERIENCE *Stan*

I come home every day at precisely 4:50 P.M. My wife, Susan, leaves work, picks up the kids at their different after-school programs, and arrives home at approximately 5:45 P.M. The timing is no accident. My wife and I made a deal years ago that if she picks up the kids, I'll have dinner on the table when the troops arrive. She hates cooking and I desperately need that one hour of quiet time to decompress from my stressful day. Without it, I don't have emotional space for anyone. Our arrangement was perfect. I got home, put on sweat pants, turned on the news, started dinner, and relaxed. When my wife and kids got home, I was ready to engage.

About a month ago my father moved in with us. When we made that decision I knew we'd have some adjustments, but I had no idea that our perfect after-work arrangement would pretty much be destroyed.

What happened that ruined the routine? Mornings go well; everyone sits down for breakfast and rushes out the door about the same time. It is a little hectic, but what family isn't in the morning? Here is where the problem arises. After everyone leaves, Stan's father is home alone for the entire day. By the time Stan gets home from work, Dad is conversation starved and wants to talk. He starts with, "So, Stanley, how was your day? Do anything interesting? Where did you eat lunch? Who did you talk to? Did you call your sister? I'm sure she'd like to say hello." Stan hasn't had his alone time and feels completely stressed out. He gets impatient with what he perceives as a litany of mindless questions. To get the quiet time he needs he sometimes hides in his bedroom and turns on the TV rather than making dinner.

Susan comes home to a cold kitchen and becomes frustrated, Stan feels guilty for reneging on their bargain, Dad feels rejected and lonely, and the kids start grabbing Pop Tarts out of the cabinet because they are "absolutely starved." The family routine is no longer intact.

There are no bad guys in this scenario, just people who have yet to successfully maneuver through the balancing act of creating new family dynamics and routines. In addition, Stan is an avoider. He clearly had a problem, but instead of opening a dialogue, he hid in his room. It may have seemed like the easy solution at the time; however, in the long run he hurt his father's feelings, made his wife angry, and gave his kids a sugar buzz. He would have to devise a better course of action.

Stan needed quiet time after work—this wasn't unreasonable. Stan's father is lonely and waited all day for his son to return from work so he could talk—also not unreasonable. As in any relationship, the key word is "compromise." To restore balance to the household, Stan cannot just mourn the old routine or artificially try to maintain it by hiding in the bedroom. He must work to create a new one that serves everyone in the family.

Stan initiated several attempts to restore the routine, but to no avail. It didn't work to ask his father to hang out in the living room until he was ready to talk. Every few minutes Stan's father would peak his head in the kitchen and say, "Ready yet?" One day, Stan asked his father if he wouldn't mind setting the table while he changed clothes from work. Stan took a little extra time changing while his father happily set the table. When Stan came to the kitchen, he turned the TV on and he and his father made dinner together—they didn't talk much, just cooked. Stan's dad had company and private time with his son and Stan had part of his routine back. Stan would have preferred to have the time in solitude, but that wasn't a possibility anymore. But it was okay, because Stan and his father figured out a way that worked for both of them.

Disruption of Privacy

You take on a great responsibility when you bring children into this world. You have the right to private conversations and meetings about key parenting decisions. Kids have the right to discuss personal matters with one or both parents. However, when you invite your parent to live with you, you may have to adjust the time when you have your private conversations.

ONE FAMILY'S EXPERIENCE *Sharon and Lisa*

I'm a single mom to my sixteen-year-old daughter, Lisa. For the last five years it has been just the two of us. We've had some rough patches, like most mothers and daughters, but overall we are close. I have a full-time job and Lisa has a full social life. To make sure she and I have at least a little time each day to talk, we have decided to try to have dinner together each night. It doesn't always work, but we do our best.

Three months ago, my father ran into financial problems and had to sell his house. I know Lisa was getting a little resentful that I spent so much time with him while he was sorting things out. I promised her that soon everything would go back to normal. As it turned out, things did not return to normal. Instead, Dad moved in with us.

I hoped it would be temporary, until he got on his feet, but only time would tell. In the meantime, my father was not only living with us, but was always hanging around vying for my attention. Lisa felt edged out, mainly because she and I had little time alone to talk. I felt stuck: I didn't want my father to feel unwelcome, but I didn't want to undo the relationship that Lisa and I worked hard to build.

Lisa was feeling resentful that her grandfather was living in their house. After all, she had her first boyfriend and couldn't even talk to her mother about him because Grandpa was always around. Sharon felt torn between her daughter and father. In addition, Sharon hadn't had a close relationship with her parents when she was young, so it had always been extra important to her that she have a good relationship with her daughter.

Dinnertime had been their time to discuss the day's activities and any problems or issues. It is important to preserve time together, but dinnertime may no longer be the right time once a parent moves in. Again, setting boundaries that protect the core family is not about disliking the housemate parent or feeling that he is intruding; it is about an important family dynamic that needs to be nurtured. To do so, you may have to juggle your schedule to figure out a time that works while honoring the fact that you now have a new family member.

It is not always easy to speak frankly, especially if you plan on asking the housemate parent to give you or your family privacy. However, avoiding the conversation will ultimately create either a blowup or such hurt feelings that no one is comfortable in the house. You don't want to exclude Grandpa or run out of the room every time he enters. You also don't want to create a scenario where your children are no longer comfortable taking about private matters. Although it may be difficult, just be honest.

If the housemate parent's mental condition or personality makes it impossible to have an open conversation, that's okay. Keep thinking until you come up with the right solution to manage the problem. Sharon felt certain that discussing problems with her father was out. So, she and Lisa did come up with their own solution that worked for them, without alienating or discussing it with Grandpa. Before Grandpa moved in, Sharon and Lisa would do the dishes immediately after dinner—that's when they would talk. After Sharon's father came to live with them, instead of doing the dishes right away, Sharon and Lisa went for a walk. Rain or shine, they get a little exercise, share their day, and spend time together. When they return home, they do the dishes and chat with Grandpa, restoring the family routine.

You, too, may have to shift time and activities to ensure alone time with your children or spouse. With a little thought, it can be done without alienating your parent.

Disruption of Internal Harmony

If you are harboring resentment and fueling negative thinking, you may be reacting to imaginary insults. Your attitude toward your parent determines whether or not you see dead ends or potential solutions to the problems that inevitably present themselves. Your attitude and pent-up emotions determine the level of family harmony.

ONE FAMILY'S EXPERIENCE *Abby and Elaine*

I wasn't thrilled when my husband, Dan, pressured me to have his mother, Elaine, or Martha Stewart as I like to call her, move in with us. I am self-conscious about my housekeeping because her house was always immaculate. I know she doesn't say anything about my mediocre housekeeping, but I can feel her thinking about it.

One morning, I walked into the kitchen to find Elaine washing dishes. I didn't mean to get angry, but it just slipped out.
I snapped, "Elaine, you may not believe this, but I can clean my
own house." She looked so stunned by my response that I felt
terrible. She replied that she just had a bowl of cereal and was
putting her dish in the dishwasher. Would I prefer she left the
dish in the sink?

Abby saw her mother-in-law washing dishes. Abby's own
insecurities and negative thinking had already reached a fever
pitch, and Abby perpetuated her own fears—that Elaine
either doesn't like her or doesn't believe she is a good wife,
mother, or housekeeper. Is that true? We have no real way
of knowing. However, we do know that Elaine's dishwash-
ing was not a commentary. At that moment, it was a simple
matter of dirty dish meets soap. Unfortunately for both of
them, Abby's insecurities and self-doubts created tension and
disruption in the house. Dan, especially, can't be comfortable
when his wife and mother aren't getting along.

After Abby's sarcastic comment to Elaine, she felt badly;
she knew she overreacted. When her husband came home
they discussed what happened, and it dawned on her: Yes,
Elaine was an amazing housekeeper, but that didn't mean
that every time Elaine tried to help around that house that
she was insinuating that Abby wasn't. She was just helping.

Elaine's life was built around being the mother of the
house, the homemaker, the hostess. Now, she no longer has
her house, her "job," and in many ways, the things that made
her happy. After talking the encounter over with her husband, Abby had an idea. Rather than fight Elaine, she would
enlist her help. Abby put her pride aside and asked Elaine if
she would mind helping her with the laundry. There were,

after all, seven people living in the house. They spent the afternoon together washing, folding, and ironing. For the first time they let their guards down, and they restored the family unity. This is not to say that the situation was permanently resolved; it wasn't. But at least Abby knew that Elaine wasn't the enemy, and that they were on the path to figuring out a way to restore peace in the house. With dedication and trying a few different things, they both knew that they could work through their differences if problems arose.

Loss of control is a big issue for all parties when an elderly parent moves in. The housemate parent loses control of some of the life and independence he had before the move. The existing family loses some of their privacy and routines. The interesting part of that is that there is actually very little in this world that you can control. You can't control the weather, the stock market, house prices, traffic, the price of gasoline, or what another person thinks, believes, or feels. You can, however, control how you react to people and situations. You can harbor anger because your father-in-law now lives with you, you can find fault with everything he says and does and even send him bad vibes when he walks by, or you can accept that this is the decision you made. Family unity is about the peaceful quality of a household. Your attitude toward your parent determines your peacefulness, which dictates what happens in the house. Different attitudes yield different outcomes to the same circumstance.

For example, your father-in-law lives with you. He is aging, and maybe his hearing is weak. Every day he turns the TV volume way too loud. How does it serve you, him, or your family to become upset and huffy each time you have to remind him to keep it down? Your aggravation keeps you from finding the solution and further affects the balance of family. Remember that your father-in-law is hard of hearing, not because he is lazy or careless, but because he is aging. If you remind yourself that he is not trying to torture you with the noise, then maybe you could come up with a loving solution that preserves family harmony.

When you build resentment you are in a constant state of internal turmoil. You are upset by anything that operates differently from how it was before the big move. Now, tell yourself it is okay that Grandpa lives with you, and that your goal is to manage situations that arise. So maybe you move his television to the game room where he can play it as loudly as he would like. Or maybe you buy him a set of comfortable earphones and let him blare away. The point is, when you accept the current situation, rather than letting anger or frustration build, you can find a reasonable resolution that works for everyone. This is not to say that you will never have to address this issue again. You probably will. That's okay; with the right attitude, you'll once again find a way to manage it.

One way to avoid building up resentment is to pinpoint what is bothering you and think about potentially favorable outcomes. Include your parent when it is appropriate. For example, you could say, "Grandpa, we are concerned that you are having a difficult time hearing the TV. We want you be able to hear it, but you can't have it too loud in the house. How would you feel about watching in your room or the game room instead of the living room? Or we would be happy to buy some great earphones. What would work for you?" There is always something to do, even if it is just accepting the situation as is.

Once you have made the decision to have your parent move in with you, you will have many occasions to remember that your family dynamic has changed.

Disruption of Respect

Most people don't mean to treat family disrespectfully; it just happens sometimes as a reaction to frustration. That's what happened between Nancy and Emily.

ONE FAMILY'S EXPERIENCE *Nancy and Emily*

My mother-in-law, Emily, loved her dog. I love my dog, too, but Emily treated Susie, her Pomeranian, like a grandchild. Unfortunately, Susie died just a couple of months after Emily moved in with me, Carl, our three kids, and our bull terrier, Buster.

Buster had medical issues, including a weak stomach. Table scraps sent him "leaking" all over the house. Since Susie the Pomeranian died, Emily had emotionally adopted Buster as her new baby. I kept reminding Emily that Buster had culinary limitations: "Mom, I know you love Buster, but if you give him table scraps he will get sick all over the house." Emily replied, "I know dear, he just looks so sweet and seems hungry, and there is nothing wrong with a little treat every now and then." I was tired of having the same conversation over and over.

One day, I had a particularly hard time at work and completely lost track of time. I picked up the kids ten minutes late. I was rushing around, completely overwhelmed, and when I got home and dashed to the kitchen to make dinner, I noticed that I tracked evidence that Buster had been eating table scraps—all over the carpet. I lost control and yelled at Emily right in front of the kids. Emily was upset and embarrassed and wouldn't leave her room for days. She felt belittled and humiliated, especially because I treated her like a child in front of her grandchildren. It took weeks for all hurt feelings to mend and for life to resume.

Nancy had every right to be angry. However, she did not handle the situation respectfully. Although Emily didn't mean harm, she ignored Nancy's request and put the dog in danger. In this particular case though, Grandmother's memory had been slowly fading. As the weeks passed, it became clearer that Emily was having a difficult time with some of life's most basic tasks as well as remembering to take her medication. It was for this very reason that Nancy and her family decided to have Emily move in with them—to help take care of her.

It was not effective to simply remind Emily not to feed the dog. Nancy's tactic of reminding and yelling didn't work. A new form of problem management was needed to protect Grandma, the family, and the dog. Ultimately, Nancy decided to bring Buster to doggy day care during the day, rather than leaving him home with Emily. After work, she picked him up and brought him home. Although Emily didn't understand why Buster wasn't home during the day, it was the best decision for everyone.

Moving an elderly parent in with you is difficult across the board. It is difficult to watch as your once-competent parent loses some of her faculties. The repercussions of that cognitive loss, such as shorter temper, irrational behavior, confusion, and forgetfulness, are also difficult to witness. Your parent did not intend to lose her independence. Think of your intentions for your later years; they are probably similar to your parent's, and do not include losing your autonomy. Remember that your parent isn't the same as before. There will be times when there is no resolution but to forgive and move on.

Respect does not mean that you give up your place as head of the household. It does not mean that you do not have the right to make rules in your own home. It does not negate that you will at times have to make difficult decisions that will make you unpopular. It does mean that you remind yourself you are all family, and that deep down your parent is living with you because you want to take care of her. You accept that, at times, it is a big sacrifice, but you don't take that out on your parent. You should never treat your parent as a child, even if she acts like one. Do not reprimand your parent in front of the grandchildren. This will be humiliating for them and uncomfortable for your children. No matter how upset you are, remember to treat your parent as you would want to be treated.

Lessons Learned

Family unity and your commitment to it can very well be the determining factor in whether or not your family's decision to have your parent move in was the right one. At any moment in time, you or your parent can make a mistake. That's fine, because in any moment you can also decide to move past it and continue working toward the goal of harmony. There are many creative ways to manage problems as they arrive. Your job is to keep an open mind and find them. Your new life will not always be perfect, but with regular and flexible problem management, clearly communicated boundaries, and recognition of each other's limitations, life with a parent can be good and can work for the whole family.

coming to terms with your decision

THERE IS A TURNING POINT for each family member when an aging parent moves in. The turning point signifies an opportunity to make a choice: You can choose to move forward and find a way to make the new extended family work or you can hold onto the past, digging your heels in while you are dragged forward kicking and screaming. A tell-tale sign of this turning point (and there will be many along the way) is that you feel overwhelmed by the new living arrangement, a parent's illness, or his behavior. You just can't take it anymore. This is decision time. What will you do?

If you choose to accept your new living arrangement and your parent as part of the household, you and your family will be able to move forward peacefully. If you continue to fight, you may continue to build anger and resentment, which could ultimately tear your family apart.

Keep an open mind, and remind yourself to see life from your parent's point of view. This will bring increased acceptance, especially if tensions run high. Acceptance of the situation will remind you of your motivation for moving your parent in the first place. You want to take care of him and have him as part of the family, especially as he continues to age. Remind yourself of your commitment to this process.

In the case of Rick and his wife, Karen, they instinctively knew that once they made the decision to move Ben in with them, there was no turning back. There was no room for regret and no bemoaning the change in their lives. Their attitude of acceptance was natural for them. Unfortunately, that is not the case for everyone.

ONE FAMILY'S EXPERIENCE *Rick and Ben*

I'm looking forward to tonight. Our plans may not seem all that special to anyone else, but they are to us. Tonight I'll be sitting in the living room with a giant bowl of popcorn, my wife, Karen, my three kids ages 6, 8, and 9, and my father-in-law, Ben, for family movie night. A year ago I couldn't imagine actually wanting to spend time like this, so I am grateful that we made it here, and that we're all together and happy.

When my wife first brought up the idea of her father moving in with us, I thought it was a good idea; we both believe in keeping our family close. However, within a week of the move, I was ready to strangle him.

When Ben first moved in, I was irritated by his possessiveness over his daughter—my wife, Karen. He was acting like a two-year-old. Every time Karen and I would get into a conversation or she would pick up the phone, we would hear her father in the other room saying, "Karen. Karen . . . where are you?" He was constantly calling her throughout the house. God forbid she would leave for a second to get the mail.

Additionally, he was always underfoot. He would just pop up everywhere I was; I was literally tripping over him. It was a little disconcerting. I am embarrassed to say that, in reaction, I found myself staying a little later at work and busying myself in the woodshop in the basement when I got home.

One day after work, about a month after Ben moved in, I just didn't want to deal with him, so I went to my woodshop to escape—and there he was, straightening up. He was organizing my tools on the peg-board wall—something I had been meaning to do. It was a nice gesture. I watched him for a minute and it suddenly clicked: This wasn't just some old guy annoying me and vying for my wife's attention; this was the man who singlehandedly raised the woman I loved. This was the man who treated me like a son since the day I proposed to his daughter. This was the man who has never forgotten a birthday—mine or the kids. And, this was the man who turned me on to woodworking and showed me unending patience as he was teaching me— Mr. Thumbs—the most basic skills. He wasn't perfect, but he did his best and was always there for Karen, me, and the kids.

It dawned on me that moving in with us was a huge change for him, too. So I asked him, "How's it going, Dad? This move has to be a big adjustment for you." His response was, "Hell yeah! I don't know if I am coming or going. I don't know what to do with myself. I feel like I am just walking around in circles." We both laughed and laughed, though part of me felt like crying. And we finally talked about everything—just like we used to.

It wasn't easy; there were some sticky times. Our lives have changed since he moved in, yet we have all settled into the new family dynamic and routine. We talk, we get on each other's nerves, and we share Karen's attention. The kids love having their grandpa around. And for the first time in years, Ben feels safe and part of a family. We love having him live with us; it makes the family complete. For us, moving Dad in was the absolute right decision—without a doubt!

Karen was happy to have her father around, but she knew it was getting difficult for Rick. She was thrilled when he finally turned the corner and relaxed into the decision. This allowed them both to press forward to create a new family dynamic including Ben, rather than fighting to preserve what once was. Movie night was one of the new routines that they all loved. The kids even brought friends over to join them. This success can be attributed to their loving relationship, similar motivations, Ben's good health, a strong core family unit, selflessness, and lots of talking. Most important, there was no blaming— just forgiveness, acceptance, and moving on.

There were hard times, but relationships of all sorts go through rocky periods. The commitment to making the relationship work is what distinguishes those that last from those that don't. Everyone in this family put in the effort to make it work, so it did.

Remind Yourself Why You Moved Your Parent In

It is easy to get caught up in the details of life and focus on what isn't working. That is a downward spiral. When you find yourself feeling angry or negative, remind yourself of your intention to care for your parent. If that is in the forefront of your mind, the details won't matter quite as much.

In addition to caring for your parent, there will also be times when the decision to move a parent in is colored with personal motives. This was the case with Peter and Kali.

ONE FAMILY'S EXPERIENCE *Peter and Kali*

My wife, Kali, and I live in a small suburb outside of Washington, D.C. We decided to bypass the conventional route of getting married and having kids; instead, during our eighteen-year relationship, we focused on our lifestyle filled with friendships, travel, personal interests, and hobbies.

Two years ago, over Thanksgiving, Kali's eighty-five-year-old father died suddenly. It was a shock to the entire family. Kali and her four brothers were deeply affected, but their mother, Nora, was completely devastated. She stopped taking care of herself, the house, and her cats. Nora lived outside of Philadelphia, several hours away from us, so Kali's four brothers stepped in to look in on their mom when they could. However, Kali wasn't sure her brothers were really taking good care of her, so every weekend Kali and I would go to Philadelphia and pick up the slack—clean her mom's house, buy groceries, take her shopping, bring her to the hairdresser, and so on.

After a few months, I started getting pretty tired of spending every weekend at Nora's, and wanted time off from work to relax, read, and go out with friends. Kali and I talked it over, and we agreed it would be alright if I stopped making the trips to Philadelphia. Kali went alone. I never dreamed it could happen to us, but over time I felt like we were drifting apart. Our weekends used to be our time for romance, friends, and adventures, and now we spent them apart. I really missed her. I needed to find a solution, so Kali and I decided it might make sense to move Nora in with us. We had the room, and this way we could resume our life.

It made sense to me at the time. Move Nora in and I will get my weekends back with Kali. That was wishful thinking. Now that Nora lives with us, we play Scrabble and cards on the weekends, dinners are no longer eat and run but sit-down in the kitchen, and we have cats everywhere. I can't remember the last time we went out to dinner alone or went hiking or spent Saturday night with friends. I have no privacy, and am clearly the odd man out in my own home. Kali and Nora are always talking and planning and cooking. I don't like feeling like low man on the totem pole of Kali's priority list, but that is where I clearly am. One of the reasons I didn't want kids was because I didn't want to end up in this position; now here I am. I have not only lost my weekends with my partner, but my weekdays and my lifestyle, too.

The death of Kali's father sent the family into a tailspin; Peter thought moving his mother-in-law in would normalize the family. His main motivation for the move was to keep Kali from leaving every weekend. He may have accomplished that, but he didn't accomplish his true goal, which was to turn back the clock to the time when he and Kali were free to do as they pleased and manage their lives and time together without familial influence. This goal, of course, was not attainable.

Moving Nora in did not produce the result that Peter wanted and he became frustrated and overwhelmed. He reached his turning point quickly. At first he chose (whether consciously or unconsciously) to hold on to the past and fight the current living situation. He did so by:

- Becoming sullen when he saw Nora and Kali together
- Refusing to play Scrabble because he would rather have been at a jazz club
- Getting annoyed by Nora's cats

- Adopting the "if you would rather be with your mother than me, then I don't need you either" attitude
- Withdrawing emotionally from his relationship with Kali
- Scowling at Nora
- Rehashing his decision to invite Nora to live with them

Peter held onto the past for weeks. He became angrier as the days went by. He could feel himself losing what he so desperately wanted to hold on to, which was his partner. He was approaching another turning point, yet there was no sign that Peter was going to make a decision to accept the current living situation. Days went by, and still no monumental epiphany. Nothing came out of the sky to show him the light. He just grew tired and gave up fighting.

Friday night rolled around, and out came the Scrabble board. Kali said, "Hey, Pete, I'm tired of beating Mom every week in Scrabble. How about joining us and giving me a run for my money." So he did; he played and had a nice time. During the game, Peter said, "Nora, Kali and my anniversary is next week. How would you feel if Kali and I went out for a romantic dinner alone?" Nora said, "I have been telling Kali I don't need a babysitter." And so there it was; life was beginning to shift.

The turning point came, and Peter unconsciously chose to relax and accept. His life didn't return to what it once was, but now it was heading in a better direction. He made peace with the decision and let go of the resentment. He also made sure that he and Kali had one night a week when they went out together. Over time, they created a new dynamic. Nora began leaving the grieving process over the loss of her husband and went to Philadelphia every now and then to visit her sons and friends. Slowly, they settled into the new arrangement, and although it wasn't perfect, it worked for them.

Lessons Learned

Moving an elderly parent in with you will change your life. The change isn't guaranteed to make your life better or worse; it's just guaranteed to make your life different than it was before the move. It doesn't matter how you came to the decision and under what circumstance: You made the decision, and here you are. What are you going to do now? You can harbor and build resentments. That decision will probably rob you and your family of happiness and the possibility of creating a new family dynamic. Or, you can live in the present and accept that this is now your life (at least temporarily). Or, you can find someplace in between, where most of us fall. It's up to you.

Think of yourself as a surfer—maneuvering the waves and handling the unexpected bumps and turns while keeping your eye on the goal of being a happy family.

Be aware of your frustrations mounting. This is the time to make your conscious decision to take a path that will bring harmony to your household. Repetitive thoughts create emotions. Rehashing, "I never should have let Dad move in—my life is ruined" will surely create anxiety that will snowball; acceptance will bring peace. In addition, you might actually enjoy having your parent around when you are no longer fighting it.

There are no set answers to the moving-in question. It is a personal decision, and whether or not it works depends largely on how you handle the changes the decision brings. Some find they feel great fulfillment having three generations living together, sharing stories, and loving and supporting one another. They enjoy working in tandem in the kitchen to make dinner or sitting on the porch watching the kids put on a show. For others, the arrangement only brings resentment, alienation, bad feelings, arguments, and the break of an emotional connection that took a lifetime to build.

The best way to avoid making the wrong decision for you is to do your homework up front. Think through the probabilities and possibilities and ask yourself, "Can I approach this move with love, compassion, and open mindedness? Do I know enough about the aging process and the condition my parent has? Am I equipped to handle it, and can I put my ego aside and get professional help when I need it? Can I go with the flow and look forward rather than wishing this never happened? How will this move affect my family?" Regardless of whether in hindsight it was the best decision or not, trust that you did the best you could at the time and you can probably make it work, even if making it work requires constant change.

Coping with an aging parent's needs is not easy. It requires the same commitment and resolve that carries a marriage through good times, tough ones, financial stress, and emotional events. Relationships are in a constant state of change and growth. It is no different with a parental relationship.

Making a relationship work with parents is difficult because of the added burden of emotional baggage from childhood and the change of roles, as well as the mental and physical deterioration that can accompany old age. You must be prepared on all levels for change, and accept (some might say resign yourself to) both the joys of your new arrangement and the mistakes you and your parents will inevitably make along the way. This acceptance can bring emotional peace and help guide you toward making the new arrangement work.

And finally, don't forget the power of saying, "I'm sorry." Human nature makes us resilient; we always have the ability to forgive and forget. However, in order to get to a better emotional place, someone usually needs to step up and forgive first. Why waste time waiting for your parent to admit to wrongdoing? You may as well begin the process of moving on from a difficult situation and apologize first. Acknowledge what you might have done better, even if it is just for the way you expressed your anger. The words, "I'm sorry" go a long way.

conclusion

THE DECISION TO CARE FOR your parent is a loving choice. You want to care for him in the best possible way. Inviting an elderly parent to move in with you has far-reaching implications. Your whole life will be affected, from financial realities to changing family dynamics, from role reassignment to safety issues, from power struggles to forgiveness and deepening closeness and respect. Your goal is to find a way for both you and your parent to respect and value each other's lives, space, and presence.

The families that moved their elderly parent into their home, in the end, all expressed gratitude that they had the opportunity to care for their parent in a very special way as well as act as a role model for their own children in terms of how to treat and care for their loved ones. In addition, the grandchildren had time to intimately get to know Grandma or Grandpa. Even if a good portion of their time together was laced with illness or difficulty, the next generation still had a unique opportunity to share their day-to-day life with their grandparent, giving them the great gift of having active daily memories they can cherish throughout their lives.

Having read through the pages of this book, you have had the opportunity to witness the journey that other families have taken. You know that no matter what your experience, you are not alone—there are millions facing similar challenges. You have read about different kinds of decisions with different outcomes. Hopefully, this glimpse into the lives of others has given you tips and strategies to help your own journey unfold a little more smoothly. Maybe after taking The Moving-In Quiz you have changed your mind about whether or not to move your parent in. Hopefully, it has strengthened your belief that you are making the right choice.

You are now armed with the right intention and the right information. Know in your heart that you are doing the best job of caring that you possibly can, and find peace in your new role as caretaker, no matter what comes your way.

glossary of eldercare terms

AARP (American Association of Retired Persons)
AARP is a nonprofit organization dedicated to providing information, resource lists, benefits, discounts, products, investment services (including financial planning, consumer protection, counseling, and tax preparation), and insurance for its members. AARP is the largest organization for people over the age of fifty, with more than 38 million members. Membership is expected to grow significantly as baby boomers age. AARP also has award-winning publications keeping its members up to date on policies, programs, and benefits that are highly relevant as one retires and ages. AARP is a wonderful resource and starting place for gathering information. Visit *www.aarp.org* for more information.

Adult day centers
Adult day centers should not be confused with senior centers. (See senior centers for more information.) Adult day centers provide daytime care and socialization for adults who need supervision or help with medication, eating, walking,

and using the restroom. They often have skilled nursing and transportation available. Many adult children caring for their elderly parent opt to send them to an adult day center while they are at work, giving their parent a chance to get out of the house. When considering an adult day center, make sure the staff is equipped to handle your parent's specific needs.

Advance directive

An advance directive is a legal document that is signed while the person is mentally competent. It outlines preferences for medical treatment. An advance directive may be in the form of a living will or durable medical power of attorney. It is used if the person is unable to communicate his/her wishes during a medical event.

ASAP (Aging Service Access Point)

ASAP exists along with other similar agencies throughout the United States. They are nonprofit organizations that provide free advice and counseling as well as subsidized services to you and your parent over the age of sixty. They access government agencies to offer an array of services such as housekeeping, meals, food shopping, personal care, and laundry. These and other services may be free or you may have a copay, depending on your parent's financial situation. The goal of these organizations is to help the elderly remain safely in their own home or in a family member's home rather than in an institution.

Asset preservation (in eldercare)

Asset preservation is the act of safeguarding assets while financially planning for long-term care.

Assets
Assets are things of value such as money, stocks and bonds, art, jewelry, or other items that have cash value.

Assisted living facilities
Assisted living facilities are communities of individual housing units, apartment or garden style. They are for people who can primarily live independently, but need some help rather than full-time skilled nursing. The range of assistance varies and is usually paid for a-la-carte. A resident usually pays a monthly fee which includes rent, housekeeping, reassurance services (see reassurance services), activities, transportation, basic utilities, two meals, and so on. Additional services can be paid for and include medication supervision, personal care, and doctor appointment supervision. Many assisted living facilities have a graduated care plan, meaning that as your parent ages and requires more intensive services, the facility is equipped to handle additional care. Some care levels go all the way to full Alzheimer's care and nursing or hospice care. Depending on the facility, some units are fully equipped with kitchens.

Beneficiaries
A beneficiary is the person or persons named as entitled to (heir) accounts, assets, proceeds, property, insurance policies, etc.

Care managers
Care managers oversee all aspects of care for an elderly person. They act as a project manager; the project being caring for your parent. There are an increasing number of home health care organizations that have expanded their services to offer care management services. Because caring for an elderly

parent can feel like a full-time job, this type of service is beneficial to the adult child who is caring for their elderly parent while trying to manage their career and home life. It is also beneficial to use this type of service if a mediator or point person is necessary to keep the peace among siblings and other family members. If you are interested in finding a good care manager to help oversee your parent's medical and emotional needs, consider contacting the National Association of Professional Geriatric Care Managers (*www.caremanagers.org*). When picking a care manager, look for one who offers more than a one-time service, who will continue to work with you throughout your role as caretaker. Some even offer a flat fee for a lifetime of services.

Care plan

A care plan is a thought-out, structured plan to use for caring for your elderly parent. It eliminates the haphazard approach to managing finances and emotional and medical care for your parent. For a care plan to be effective, it must evolve as your parent's needs change.

Companion reassurance services

Companion reassurance services are a telephone check-in service that calls your parent daily to make sure that he/she is okay, to chat, and to offer a warm, though brief, conversation. Many churches, synagogues, and other volunteer agencies offer companion reassurance services. The volunteers are usually senior citizens themselves, making it a mutually beneficial phone call. This service is helpful for the busy adult child responsible for an aging parent's care. The adult child is also reassured by knowing that their parent has social contact beyond what he/she can provide.

Contact list

A contact list includes important phone numbers of family members, doctors, and other important phone numbers that may need to be referenced in case of an emergency.

Continuing care retirement communities

Continuing care retirement communities (CCRC) have housing, health care, and social services at a single location. They are mainly nonprofits, funded by religious organizations. There are many different types of CCRCs; however, there are basic similarities. Once a person moves in and pays an entry fee, as long as monthly fees are paid, he/she can stay for the duration of his/her life, regardless of an increase in medical needs. An entrance fee can be anywhere from $50,000 to $200,000. Monthly fees vary from $1,000 to $6,000 per month. A resident can choose an all-inclusive care monthly fee, which will be higher than a-la-carte costs, for service fees. Services range from light personal care help to full-time skilled nursing. As with a nursing home, if you are considering this option, it is best to do your homework ahead of time and look into several.

DNR (Do Not Resuscitate)

A DNR request is a petition that dictates that a patient should not be resuscitated if his/her heart and lungs have failed. DNR only applies to CPR (cardiopulmonary resuscitation), when your heart and lungs are no longer functioning properly. It does not apply to other forms of lifesaving interventions. Many people mistake DNR orders for no heroic measures or advance directive orders. They are not the same. DNRs are usually done in writing, although a patient can give a verbal DNR order to his/her doctor personally. However, it is always best to have it in writing. Patients usually initiate a DNR order when they are terminal and do not want their lives artificially maintained.

Durable power of attorney
A durable power of attorney is a document that allows a person to act on someone's behalf even if the grantor becomes disabled or incapacitated. Sometimes an advance directive or health-care directive is included in the durable power of attorney to ensure the person's health-care wishes are honored. (See Power of Attorney below.)

Eldercare law
Eldercare law is the practice of law that concentrates on issues pertaining to the elderly. Eldercare law includes topics such as asset preservation, estate planning, wills, and advocacy work.

Estate planning
Estate planning is the organization, administration, and disposition of assets, wills, health care directives, and trusts.

Estate tax minimization trust
Estate tax minimization trusts are trusts set up to reduce inheritance tax for beneficiaries.

Executor
Usually referring to a will, an executor is the person who has been given the task of carrying out the directions and intentions of a will. The executor is selected by the person who is writing their will, known as the testator. The executor is responsible for disbursing property to the assigned beneficiaries, locating potential heirs, arranging debt payment

including estate taxes, and collection of debts owed to the estate. The executor can have a difficult job, especially if family members are not happy with the will or are combative. When there is a large estate to be disbursed, the executor may run into a situation where those not entitled to benefit try to claim as though they are. The executor is also faced with the daunting task of defending the will if it is being contested.

Financial planning

Financial planning is the phrase describing a comprehensive money management effort that includes budgeting, insurance, wills, tax planning, and retirement planning.

Geriatric care manager

Geriatric care managers, also known as care managers, act as a project manager for your parent's needs. They oversee the process of orchestrating services and care for your parent. If you are interested in finding a good care manager to help oversee your parent's medical and emotional needs, consider contacting the National Association of Professional Geriatric Care Managers (*www.caremanagers.org*).

Graduated care plan

Graduated care plans take into consideration the progression of needs that might apply to your parent. For example, many assisted living facilities have a graduated care plan for their residents so as your parent ages and needs more services, the facility is ready and able to comply.

Guardianship

A guardianship is a legal process where the courts determine if someone is unable to act on his/her own behalf, and therefore appoints someone else to manage his/her affairs and decisions. A family member usually petitions to be granted guardianship.

Health-care proxy
A health-care proxy is a legal document that assigns health care decisions to another person if you are unable to make decisions on your own (e.g., if you are in a coma or mentally unable to make a clear and rational decision). A health-care proxy is not the same as a living will.

Home health care
Home health care is a range of care services that are supplied to the elderly living in the home—either theirs or yours. Many adults who have moved an aging parent into their home hire home health care workers to care for their parent while they are at work or to do more personal caretaking tasks such as bathing or administering some medication.

Home sharing
Home sharing is when two or more senior citizens, usually friends, agree to rent or buy a home together. It is most common among single or widowed women who enjoy company, sharing tasks, caregiving to each other, and dividing financial burdens.

Hospice care
Hospice care is only for those who are terminally ill and require constant care and pain management. It is typically offered by hospitals and long-term care facilities as well as other hospice organizations. Hospice focuses on symptom management and control, not curing. Hospice care is not only for the elderly, but for anyone facing the end of life.

Informal caregivers

Informal caregivers (a large majority of the elderly receive this kind of care) are family and friends who support and care for an aging relative. The informal caregiver tends not to have formal training or experience, but offers help allowing the person to either remain in their own home or in the home of another family member.

Irrevocable trust

An irrevocable trust is a trust set up so it cannot be changed or altered in any way without the consent of the beneficiaries. (See trusts.)

Living will

A living will is a document that lets family and medical caregivers know what types of lifesaving measures you approve. And it allows the grantor to decide who will be in charge of ensuring his/her wishes are carried out.

Long-term care facility

See nursing home.

Long-term care insurance

Long-term care insurance covers nursing home and other care services for people unable to care for themselves. Long-term care can cost anywhere from $100 to $200 or more per day. The insurance itself can cost anywhere from $100 to $12,000 per year depending on age and benefit options. Therefore, unless the person has saved a great deal of money long-term care insurance may be a good option. Long-term care insurance picks up where health insurance, Medicare, and Medicaid fall short.

Minor trusts
Minor trusts are created to hold assets for a minor child until he/she reaches the age designated by the donor. The donor's designated age doesn't have to be eighteen or twenty-one. For example, a grandparent can create a minor trust to leave money for his grandchild to receive once she reaches the age of twenty-five.

Meal services
Meal services (such as Meals on Wheels) is a community- or private-charity based organization that brings food to the elderly for a very small fee. The Meals on Wheels website is *www.mowaa.org.*

Medicaid
Medicaid is a federal/state welfare program that is designed to pay for a range of care such as medical, nursing home, and home health aides for those who are unable to pay for it themselves. There are strict requirements for eligibility such as age, income, assets, health, and family status. Visit the U.S. Department of Health & Human Services website (*www.hhs .gov*) for more information.

Medicare
Medicare is a federal program for those over the age of sixty-five or for those with certain disabilities.

National council on aging (NCOA)
NCOA is a national organization that offers a wealth of information on all aging-related issues. They have lists of professional resources and programs. They also have publications and online support (*www.ncoa.org*).

Nursing home

A nursing home, also known as a long-term care facility, skilled nursing facility, convalescence home, or rest home, is only for those who require constant nursing care and who cannot perform daily activities such as eating, bathing, or walking without assistance. Nursing home patients do not require hospitalization but cannot live without constant supervision.

Ombudsman

An ombudsman is the person who works with residents or their families who reside in nursing homes and long-term care facilities to investigate and resolve complaints. The ombudsman is the advocate for the elderly.

PACE (Program for All Inclusive Care for the Elderly)

PACE, along with other similar programs, was created to offer assistance for the elderly who need care but still want to live at home for as long as possible. However, PACE staff will also supply supplemental services for those in an assisted living facility. They offer a wide array of services such as home health aides, medication supervision, adult day health, transportation, etc. Income is the determining factor behind payment for services. PACE works with Medicare, Medicaid, and sliding-scale payment options for those paying directly.

Palliative care

Palliative care is care that offers emotional, physical, and spiritual comfort. It does not aim to cure. Many confuse hospice care with palliative care. Hospice care is the organized program for delivering palliative care. The goal of palliative care is to make the terminally ill patient as comfortable as possible in their own homes.

Power of attorney

A power of attorney is a document that allows a person who has been given power of attorney (POA) to act legally and financially on behalf of another (who gave POA) unless the giver becomes incapacitated. A durable power of attorney remains intact whether or not the person becomes incapacitated. (See durable power of attorney.)

Probate

Probate is the act of testing or reviewing a will to ensure its authenticity. It is also the act of carrying out the will's directives and disbursing assets.

Respite care

Respite care is short-term care that gives the caregiver a short break from the stress and burden of caring for an elderly parent. This care can take place in the patient's home or off site in another facility. In most cases, respite care is not covered by any insurance; fortunately, there are volunteer services that offer this type of either overnight or one- or two-day care options. There are national organizations set up to help the caregiver receive the help he/she needs (*www.respitelocator.org*).

Reverse mortgage

A reverse mortgage is for the elderly person who owns their own home and is equity rich, yet cash poor. Available in every state in the country, it is a loan against equity that pays the borrower a lump sum, a monthly installment, or in some cases provides an equity line of credit that can be used as needed. There are two unusual features of the reverse mortgage. The first is that it does not have to be repaid for as long the borrower lives in the home. Upon selling, moving, or death, the loan must be paid in full. Second, the reverse mortgage usually ensures the borrower a lifetime of tenancy in the home. In other words, they will never lose their home because of the mortgage. However, even after you take out a reverse mortgage you obligated to pay taxes, insurance, and maintenance. You still own the home. The amount of money you receive monthly depends on the borrower's age, amount of equity in the home, and cost of loan repayment. There are many different reverse mortgages. The costs of the loan can be the determining factor in how much you receive each month. Look into several and compare costs and features.

Revocable trusts

A revocable trust is a trust that can be altered at any time during the grantor's lifetime. Therefore, the assets within the trust are taxable and considered the grantor's property until his/her death. (See trusts.)

Retirement communities

Retirement communities should not be confused with assisted living facilities. Retirement communities are for active, healthy adults who wish to live in an environment surrounded by their peers. These communities usually have social centers, exercise facilities and pools, dining rooms, activities, cultural and educational events, shuttle services, and so on. Some also have a graduated care option, which allows the resident to stay as they age whether or not their health deteriorates and they ultimately need more care. Usually, these communities have separate sections, depending on the level of care you need. They are careful to keep independent clientele separate from those needing more assistance.

Senior apartments

Senior apartments are apartments for those fifty-five and older. They range from basic market rates and below to high-end luxury units. They are constructed and geared toward the elderly and can provide transportation, social services, and other support. However, they are for independent seniors. If your parent needs assistance, senior apartments may not be the right solution unless you provide the additional care either personally or by hiring a home health aide.

Senior centers

Senior centers should not be confused with adult day centers. Senior centers are a social and entertainment center for seniors who are alert and relatively active and who do not need supervision or care. Senior centers can provide meals, but they do not provide medical supervision or assistance. Your active, healthy parent will feel much more comfortable surrounded by other healthy adults rather than in an adult center with others who are less independent. Many towns and cities sponsor senior centers and are free to residents. However, privately sponsored senior centers can cost anywhere from $50 to $300 annually.

Skilled nursing facility

See nursing home.

Spendthrift trust

A spendthrift trust is a trust that is put in place for someone who the grantor believes cannot handle their finances. A trustee controls the trust, giving money to the beneficiary or even just paying bills and creditors, completely bypassing the beneficiary himself/herself.

Supplemental needs trust

Supplemental needs trusts are created for a person who already receives state or federal aid. An inheritance could potentially disqualify the person from receiving his/her government aid, so a supplemental needs trust is established to give help in addition to the aid, not instead of it. The funds from the trust would supply supplemental help when needed.

Trusts

There are many different kinds of trusts. However, in the basic legal trust an individual gives control over assets to an institution (the trust) to benefit the beneficiaries.

Veterans benefits (VA)

Veterans benefits is nontaxable money paid to an eligible veteran or his/her spouse. The purpose is to either supplement or pay for services such as home health care, an assisted living facility, visiting nurse, or nursing home.

Volunteer companions

Volunteer companions, usually town or religious-group sponsored, have volunteers who either visit senior citizens or accompany them grocery shopping or to the doctor's office.

Wills

A will is a legal document that clearly defines a person's wishes for dispersing assets, beneficiaries, naming executors, and paying final bills and debts. A will is always probated unless all assets are dispersed prior to death.

appendix b
additional resources

THERE ARE MANY potential resources available as you begin the responsibility of caring for your elderly parent. The following is just the tip of the iceberg. Ask your doctor for support groups, local agencies, and nonprofit organizations that can continue to steer you in the right direction. There are also many care-management organizations that can potentially oversee the eldercare process.

Books on Caring for the Elderly

Delehanty, Hugh and Elinor Ginzler. *Caring for Your Parents: The Complete AARP Guide.* (New York: Sterling Publishers, 2005).

Gans, Stephen and Bruce Cohen. *The Other Generation Gap: The Middle-Aged and Their Aging Parents.* (Boston: Shambala, 1988).

Levin, Nora Jean. *How to Care for Your Parents: A Practical Guide to Eldercare.* (New York: W.W. Norton & Company, 1997).

Loverde, Joy. *The Complete Eldercare Planner: Where to Start, Which Questions to Ask, and How to Find Out.* (New York: Random House, 2009)

Manning, Doug. *Aging is a Family Affair: Planning the care of elderly loved ones.* (Oklahoma City: Insight Books, 1998).

Somers, Marion. *Elder Care Made Easier: Dr. Marion's 10 Steps to Help You Care for an Aging Loved One.* (Omaha, Nebraska: Addicus Books, 2006).

Books on Dealing with Difficult Parents

Brown, Nina. *Children of the Self-absorbed: A Grown-Up's Guide to Getting over Narcissistic Parents.* (Oakland, CA: New Harbinger Publications, 2001).

Hotchkiss, Sandy. *Why Is It Always about You: The Seven Deadly Sins of Narcissism.* (New York: Free Press, 2002).

Lebow, Grace and Barbara Kane. *Coping with Your Difficult Older Parent.* (New York: Harper Collins, 1999).

Books on Long-Term Care Insurance Options

Shelton, Phyllis. *Long-Term Care: Your Financial Planning Guide 2007.* (Hendersonville TN: LTCI Publishing, 2007).

Protection for the Elderly Websites

The National Association of Area Agencies on Aging, *www.n4a.org*, (202-872-0888)

Financial and Legal Resource Websites

National Academy of Elder Law Attorneys, *www.naela.org*, (520-881-4005)

National Association of Area Agencies on Aging, *www.n4a .org*, (202-872-0888)

The Division of Medical Assistance, *www.ncdhhs.gov*

Websites helping individuals draft wills, health care proxies, advanced directive, and so on, *www.legalzoom.com, www .lawmart.com, www.livingtrustsontheweb.com*

General Eldercare Resource Websites

www.elderindustry.com

www.drmarion.com

Eldercare Websites

Eldercare Locator, *www.eldercare.gov*, (800-677-1116)

Family Caregiver Alliance/National Center on Caregiving, *www.caregiver.org*, (800-445-8106)

NCOA (National Council on Aging) is a national organization that supplies information on all aging related issues in addition to listings of professional resources and programs. *www.ncoa.org*, (202-479-1200)

National Alliance for Caregiving, *www.caregiving.org*

Alzheimer's Association, *www.alz.org*, (800-272-3900)

Senior Resource Center, *www.helpingelders.com*, (888-869-6295)

Aging Parents and Elder Care, *www.aging-parents-and-elder-care.com*

American Association of Retired Persons, *www.aarp.org*

Prescription and Drug Discount Websites

As most aging Americans are aware, the cost of prescription drugs can be crippling, with or without health-insurance coverage. There are options available to help senior citizens with the cost of needed medication. The following list is just a starting point.

www.helpingpatients.org

www.pillbot.com (This website lists generic brands of pharmaceuticals that may replace more expensive name brands.)

www.rxassist.org (This website lists the many drug companies that offer free or discount prescriptions for low-income people.)

Government Agencies

www.medicaid.gov

www.medicare.gov

eldercare checklists

MANY FAMILIES WHO BEGIN to care for an elderly parent in addition to their own families become overwhelmed as they try to organize their new life. Use the checklists on the following pages to ensure that you have your bases covered. Fill in these assessments and bring them with you when you speak to your parent's doctors. Your knowledge of your parent's condition and your contribution to the visit will be invaluable as the doctor determines what type of care will best serve your parent.

DAILY LIVING QUESTIONNAIRE

Task	Yes	Yes with Help	No
Can your parent stand from a seated position?			
Can your parent walk unassisted with a walker or cane?			
Can your parent dress and undress?			
Can your parent bathe and wash?			
Can your parent use the toilet?			
Can your parent prepare meals and eat?			
Can your parent take medication independently, including insulin?			
Can your parent perform diabetes blood testing (if applicable)?			
Can your parent remember to take medication?			
Can your parent tidy her room? Do laundry?			
Can your parent go grocery shopping?			
Can your parent use the telephone or call for assistance?			
Can your parent manage her money and pay bills?			
Can your parent manage her schedule (make appointments)?			
Can your parent drive?			

Notes

_____

_____

PHYSICAL AND EMOTIONAL WELL-BEING QUESTIONNAIRE			
Task	*Good*	*Fair*	*Poor*
How is your parent's memory?			
How is your parent's clarity of thought?			
How is your parent's cognitive ability?			
How is your parent's decision-making process?			
How is your parent's state of mind? Is she depressed?			
How is your parent's vision?			
How is your parent's hearing?			
How is your parent's speech?			
How is your parent's mobility?			
How are your parent's bladder and bowel control?			
How is your parent's heart/blood pressure/ cholesterol health?			
How is your parent's joint function? Arthritis?			

Notes

_____

_____

_____

_____

_____

_____

_____

ENVIRONMENTAL SAFETY AND COMFORT QUESTIONNAIRE

Task	Okay as Is	Change Required
Well-lit entryways, hallways, and rooms		
Easy-to-reach light switches		
Nonskid strips in the bathtub or shower		
Nonslip bath mats		
Sturdy handrails		
Tacked-down rug edges and corners		
Stairs and hallways clutter free		

Notes

_____

_____

_____

_____

_____

_____

_____

_____

_____

_____

_____

_____

_____

FINANCIAL INDEPENDENCE AND PREPAREDNESS QUESTIONNAIRE

Task	Yes	No
Can your parent make deposits?		
Can your parent balance her checkbook?		
Can your parent pay her bills?		
Is your parent aware of her monthly income and expenses?		
Is your parent able to file her taxes?		
Does your parent have a will?		
Has your parent assigned a power of attorney?		
Does your parent have a health-care proxy or living will?		
Was your parent or her spouse a veteran?		
Are your parent's assets organized and definable?		
Is your parent interested in setting up a trust?		
Has your parent had any estate planning?		
Does your parent have a DNR or other advanced directives?		
Does your parent have long-term care insurance?		

Notes

_____

_____

_____

_____

_____

_____

Organizational Lists

In addition to financial statements, consider keeping a list of important documents and their locations, a list of banks, creditors, and investments with account numbers and phone numbers as well as other important contacts.

DOCTOR LIST		
Doctor	*Type*	*Address/phone number*

Notes

_____

_____

_____

_____

_____

_____

PROFESSIONALS (LAWYER, ACCOUNTANT, INSURANCE AGENT, ETC.)

Name	Type	Address/phone number

Notes

_____

_____

_____

_____

_____

_____

_____

_____

BANKS AND FINANCIAL INSTITUTIONS		
Name	Type/Account Number	Address/phone number

Notes

_____

_____

_____

_____

_____

_____

_____

DOCUMENTS	
Document Type	*Location*

Notes

_____

_____

_____

_____

_____

_____

_____

Medication

Consider keeping an up-to-date list of medications and dosages on hand. It is also useful to include the purpose of the medication, the prescribing doctor, and when it will need to be refilled. This information will be helpful in case your parent is admitted to the hospital or he/she changes doctors.

MEDICATION				
Medication Name	Purpose	Dosage	Prescribing Doctor	Refill Date

Notes

_____

_____

_____

_____

_____

appendix d
your parent's financial statement

MOST PEOPLE DO NOT enjoy accounting or budgeting; however, it is a crucial step when caring for your parent. Most agencies that offer financial assistance or services will require a financial statement prior to providing services. It is also important when deciding how much your parent can contribute to the newly formed household.

FINANCIAL STATEMENT	
Income Source	*Monthly Dollar Amount*
Social Security	
Pension	
Interest Income	
Total Income	$
Expense Source	*Monthly Dollar Amount*
Mortgage	
Utilities	
Telephone	
Household supplies	
Personal products	
Credit card debt	
Loans	
Health insurance	
Auto expenses	
Food	
Clothing	
Transportation	
Gifts	
Restaurants and entertainment	
Knitting supplies	
Vacation	
Taxes	
Medical and prescription copays	
Professional services	
Dry cleaning	
Subscriptions and memberships	
Vet	
Pet food and supplies	
Senior center	
Misc.	
Total Expenses	$
Money Left Over (Income – Expenses)	$

Your Parent's Financial Statement

FINANCIAL STATEMENT	
Assets	Dollar Amount
Sale of house	
Retirement in Money Market	
Stocks and bonds	
Cash on hand	
Personal property	
Total Assets	

Notes

_____

_____

_____

_____

_____

_____

_____

_____

_____

_____

_____

_____

_____

_____

_____

_____

_____

_____

index

About the Authors

David Horgan is an award-winning medical educator, promoter, filmmaker, and writer. His internationally distributed medical education titles were awarded the Freddie award for excellence in interactive education by the American Medical Association. His other writer/producer honors include a Silver Cindy, a Bronze Cindy, and being named a finalist for the American Medical Association/Time Inc. Award for his Health Education Cardio-Vascular Disease interactive education program.

Horgan's twenty-year experience includes writing and producing educational materials for elders and their families. Horgan has produced more than 100 interactive medical CD-ROM programs as well as national broadcast work with MTV and VH1. He has also produced the opening for the television show *The Fresh Prince of Bel-Air*, featuring Will Smith, on NBC.

Horgan currently lives in Western Massachusetts with his wife, three sons, and his mother-in-law.

Shira Block, MA Psychology and Counseling, a popular lecturer, writer, author, life coach, and gifted communicator, captivates audiences with her intelligent humor, clarity, and ability to pinpoint problems and devise effective solutions. Since 1991, she has taught thousands the art of effective communicating, interpersonal interacting, improving family dynamics, and effective business writing and communicating. Her workshops and personal coaching are results oriented, leaving participants with a clear path of what to do.

She has published two books: *The Way Home* and *Step-by-Step Miracles: A Practical Guide to Achieving Your Dreams* (Kensington Publishing). She currently lives in Western Massachusetts with her husband and daughter.